BRIEF
HISTORY
of *Cuba*

BRIEF HISTORY

HISTORY

of Cuba

Julio Le Riverend

Editorial José Martí

Original title in Spanish: *Breve historia de Cuba*
Edition: Mayda Argüelles and Martha Acosta
Design: Enrique Mayol
Desktop publishing: Beatriz Roussó

© 1997, Julio Le Riverend
© 1997, Carmen González
© 1997, Editorial JOSÉ MARTÍ

First reprint, 2000
Second reprint, 2006

ISBN 959-09-0109-3

INSTITUTO CUBANO DEL LIBRO
Editorial JOSÉ MARTÍ
Publicaciones en Lenguas Extranjeras
Calzada No. 259 e/ J e I, Vedado
Ciudad de La Habana, Cuba
E-mail: editjosemarti@ceniai.inf.cu
Impreso en Colombia - Printed in Colombia
Impresión: Nomos S.A.

CONTENTS

FOREWORD

A reading of this book's first edition evinces that current historical circumstances have surpassed the ones prevailing at the time of its writing. However what was written then was not the result of an undeveloped idea, but of the analysis that matched those circumstances. To issue a second edition was the obvious thing to do for, if changes were not needed or brought about at that previous stage in Cuba's internal order, the extent and nature of changes that must be made—and are, in fact, under way—in current circumstances, brought about by the big centers of power and their discrepancies, should also be appraised. In short, an in-depth study about the effects of active reality is needed, in order to attain a more precise understanding of the issues and principles that govern the Cuban society. For that active reality is open to an all-encompassing analysis of each and every problem that requires a more complex scrutiny, as befits the countless of causes and effects that have acquired a global dimension, according to the age-old project launched by the big economic centers, and to the consequences of power over society at large and over the various social groups.

This book does not merely contain the author's lineal viewpoint, but also the objective requirements which have a protagonic role within the Revolution's project. The historical importance of social services accessible to all in the context of the Revolution would suffice to realize that the project's existence is not ephemeral, but rather an offensive against the goals of domination that attempt to obliterate the entire history of essential developments during the 19th and the 20th century.

The changes we refer to reproduce themselves—or at least purport to—at an overwhelming scale worldwide. The idea is to de-rationalize traditions, eradicate the ideas and the adjustments to be made, according to a specific, rational, endogenous understanding of economic, social and political problems. This brings to the forefront two new elements, currently perceived as the response movements' reply to the global domination project mentioned in the paragraph above, highlighted by its spokesmen as the world's ultimate response in the quest of principles for a dignified coexistence. These elements are no less than the organization and dynamics of the world's objective advance against them who only envisage the infinite growth of their wealth.

Although it appears as the epitome of effective responses to the project for domination in southeast Asia in the first (1978) edition, from the current vantage point, and faced by the imminent threat of its progress, the possibility of forming new alliances, albeit more or less ephemeral, and of creating solid foundations, must be prioritized.

The first warning we should heed when approaching this issue, is that as it has often happened throughout history, the essential processes of social formation are thwarted, prevented or obstructed by countless interferences, or by the appearance of unforeseen variables, that seem to have appeared suddenly, instead of having undergone successive stages of development. From this viewpoint, this brief book could become, like the author wanted its first edition to be, a road toward the knowledge not only of what is rational and historical, but also of what appears to be sudden and unexpected. Consequently, its contents were not nourished by data or by reflections about what happened; like a bibliography carefully put together, it rather intends to expand knowledge, to shape criteria and to promote thinking based on a substantial historical logic, as truthful and coherent as possible, about what was, is and will be possible to measure in the repercussions and consequences of the 1953-1959 revolution, and of its more remote background.

PART I

16TH AND 17TH CENTURIES

Conquistadors and Indians
Beginnings of the Colonial Economy
The Colonial Society

A sad land this one, under tyranny and seigniory.[1]

MIGUEL VELÁZQUEZ

1. The Cuban-born priest Miguel Velázquez, of mixed Indian and
Spanish descent, in a letter to the King of Spain, 1528.

A map of the world will help us understand why the discovery of the Americas had such profound consequences. No other continents but Europe and Asia were known before 1492. It was not easy to reach the New World, for prejudices, conflicting interests, fears and ignorance had to be overcome first. When Christopher Columbus (1451?-1506) discovered the Americas and Cuba in 1492, he had already undergone numerous seafaring and economic experiences.

Columbus was a skilled and ambitious seaman, born in Genoa, in Italy. Before he discovered the Americas, he had sailed along the coasts of Africa, engaged in the slave trade and in various other business endeavors. Like other Europeans in his time, he did not know that, beyond the Atlantic Ocean, there existed a huge mass of land that would be called the Americas in years to come. Therefore, he requested from Fernando and Isabel, the Catholic King and Queen of Spain, that they sponsor an expedition to Asia—with whose useful products European were well acquainted—crossing the Atlantic. The king and queen agreed to support the expedition and signed a contract with Columbus stipulating an the share of the benefits from the trade carried out with that rich continent. Thus, a small fleet of three caravels—fast, light sailing ships—was organized.

On October 27, 1492, Columbus landed in Cuba, on the northern coast of the former province of Oriente. The first Indians who saw his ships fled to the hinterland. Columbus sent two of his men for a reconnaissance of the area where they had landed. Upon their return, they said they had found an abandoned Indian village whose inhabitants had disappeared, temporarily abandoning their homes and cultivated fields, as if they suspected the strangers' intentions.

The Spaniards did not embark on the conquest of Cuba until many years later. They had found much gold—which they coveted, and was scarce in Cuba—, on other islands they had discovered at the time (currently known as the Dominican Republic, Haiti and Puerto Rico). The conquistadors seized the land where the Indians lived on these islands, and made them work as their slaves. The Indians died from fatigue, assassinated by the greedy invaders or from new diseases—like smallpox—brought to the Americas by the Europeans.

The Europeans ascertained they had come to civilize the Indians, to acquaint them with Christian truth and virtues; but soon the Indians in Santo Domingo realized that was a lie. They had come to deprive them of their possessions and to make them work until they died from exhaustion. The Indians rebelled and the conquistadors redoubled their cruelty toward them, for all conquerors become infuriated when the peoples they subdue turn against them.

Diego Velázquez (1465-1524), the man entrusted with the task of conquering Cuba, was one of the most outstanding exploiters and pursuers of Indians in Santo Domingo. He and the contingent under his command, landed on the Cuba's eastern region late in 1509, some seventeen years after the discovery of the Americas.

The conquistadors who arrived in Cuba were armed with swords, steel spears and firearms, and protected their bodies with suits of armor. The Indians only had sticks, stones, arrows and the long, pointed wooden spears called assagais, which they threw from a distance against their enemies. Technically speaking, the conquistadors' weapons were much better than the Indians'. Furthermore, history teaches that conquistadors have always profited from scientific advances to manufacture more efficient weapons to be used against the peaceful people they aim to rule. That happened then in Cuba, in all of the Americas, and later in Asia and Africa.

With their firearms and their swords, the conquistadors crossed Cuba's territory, seizing Indian villages by storm. They said they civilized and converted them thus to Christianity. But the use of force, abuses and crime only sparked the peoples' indignation and hate, and the wish to free themselves from the rulers' yoke. Like the American Indians, many other colonized peoples have faced their oppressors, the men who plunder their riches.

The Indians in Cuba

There were some one hundred thousand Indians on the island when the Spanish conquistadors arrived in Cuba. They were divided into three groups. The *taínos* mainly lived in the territory occupied nowadays by the provinces of Ciego de Ávila, Camagüey, Las Tunas, Granma, Holguín, Santiago de Cuba and Guantánamo. They were the most advanced group, for they cultivated certain plants, like yucca, tobacco and cotton, and also manufactured clay utensils; they had discovered a very ingenious way to make *casabe*, which was their staple diet. They used sour yucca—which contains a powerful poison—, grated it with a *guayo*—a grater—and placed the mass thus obtained in a *sibucán*, where they squeezed the poisonous substance out of it. They shaped the dough with their hands into thin, large crackers of a sort, which they toasted over hot stones. Casabe is still made using a technique similar to that of the Indians not only in Cuba, but in other Caribbean countries, like Venezuela. Social differences had begun to appear in taíno communities between

17

those who wielded power, and those who did not; but this was only an embryo of social hierarchies.

The second Indian group, called *subtaíno*, was scattered islandwide. They hunted and fished, and lived in villages usually on the river banks or along the coast. It is possible that they were already making crude clay utensils and had begun to practice agriculture.

The *guanahatabeyes*—the third group—, lived mainly in caves in the Pinar del Río area. They were a more ancient but less advanced culture. They made a few stone tools and fed on the wild fruit they picked up, and on the animals they hunted.

Research work currently under way is aimed at characterizing the main pre-Columbian indigenous societies in Cuba; that work has brought to light new elements that will contribute to expand our knowledge about those societies. Recent archaeological findings show that the Indians had arrived in Cuba before our era. The ancient *ciboneyes* are currently divided into two groups called *Cayo Redondo* (A.D. 1) and *Guayabo Blanco* (4000-2000 B.C.), and another more ancient one has recently been discovered, that dates back to some 6000 years B.C., and has been temporarily called *Levisa*. In regard to the taínos and subtaínos, they appeared approximately in the years 1200 and 700 A.D. It will be possible, in the near future, to learn much more about the various indigenous cultures that existed in Cuba in the 15th century.

None of these peoples could resist the conquistadors' onslaught for long, but they nevertheless tried to. A small group of Indians commanded by Hatuey confronted Diego Velázquez and his troop, but were persecuted and cruelly annihilated. Hatuey was burned alive at the stake by the conquistadors. Years later, the Indian cacique Guamá succeeded in keeping resistance alive for one decade.

Some Spaniards realized that the conquest was an unspeakable crime and protested against it, arguing that the Indians were as human as the Europeans and should remain free men, able to work for themselves instead of being exploited with impunity. The Spanish friar Bartolomé de Las Casas (1474-1566) was a tireless defender of the rights of the Indians; the conquistadors, who wanted to enslave the indigenous peoples, immediately took action against him. Las Casas may be considered as the first consistent opponent of the conquest. It must not be forgotten that among the peoples where conquistadors emerge, there are also men who stand against colonialism.

The Conquistadors Seize the Island

The Spanish conquistadors founded seven towns, all of which are major cities nowadays. They were usually located near the sea, to facilitate trading with Spain. But the conquistadors also looked for areas where there were larger Indian populations whom they forced to work for them.

Every time the Spaniards founded a new town, they divided the land, the Indians and the gold mines among themselves. Work at the mines was specially hard for the Indians, for they toiled from dawn till dusk in the rivers, up to their waists in the water, without any food, washing the sand to separate the gold mixed with it. Men, women and children were engaged in these harsh tasks and, as a logical consequence, many of them died and others committed suicide to stop the sufferings caused by such merciless exploitation. Other groups of Indians were given away to the conquistadors as farmhands; a small number of Indians manufactured the casabe bought by ships that sailed across the Caribbean sea, bound for other lands. On the other hand, Indians were also destined to look after the cattle in the conquistadors' large estates. The cattle, brought into Cuba by the Spaniards, had bred freely on the Cuban countryside, and the Indians tracked them down and gathered them in safe places, thus contributing to further the economic interests of the group of big landowners, established shortly after the conquest. The conquistadors had taken over the land, the mines, the wild cattle, and the sales of casabe; it was by exploiting the Indians that they amassed their fortunes, contributing only their weapons and their might.

The towns then founded looked very poor. They were, in fact, clusters of bohíos—small cabins made with planks or canes and thatched with dry palm leaves—, scattered at random over a wild tract of land. But after the small group of conquistadors had taken over the land, enslaved the Indians and amassed a certain amount of wealth, houses made of stone and other more lasting materials began to be built. Usually, stone fortresses and castles were the first to be built, destined to defend the Spanish domains, threatened by other European colonialists; then came the churches and also the houses where the members of the city council—then called Cabildo—met. The Castillo de la Fuerza in Havana, and the Castillo de El Morro, in Santiago de Cuba, were the first built by the Spanish authorities, some four hundred years ago. They have undergone various alterations since then, but their construction began in the 16th century.

Wealth and political power at a local level were concentrated on a small group of settlers, a veritable oligarchy. With the power invested upon them by their posts in the city council—the Cabildo—, these rulers made up laws that suited their own interests. For example, they set up taxes; regulated the work to be done by Indians and blacks, whether they were free men or slaves; distributed the land, keeping the best and largest estates for themselves, and giving other Spaniards smaller farms; fixed the prices of goods to benefit the merchants and, in short, controlled life in the city and in the surrounding countryside.

The governor, appointed by the King of Spain, had authority over the Cabildos. Governors were responsible for military and repressive affairs in the colony, supervised the city councils and solved disputes among the rich. Due to the fact that the Spanish government's seat was in faraway Madrid, complaints put forth by Indians, blacks, poor Spaniards and poor natives or criollos remained unheard by the metropolitan colonial authorities. Thus, colonial governors and their protegees were the true lords and masters of the entire island. They were generally allied with the Spanish settlers or with Cuban natives who owned large estates or did business with the powers that be.

Black Slaves

Harsh work and mass murders decimated the Indians and, to replace them, the conquistadors began to bring African slaves into the island. Africans were crowded into ships by the hundreds, barely able to move, and brought across the Atlantic to be sold in any of the American colonies to big landowners and other wealthy people, who forced them to work non-stop. Merchants from all "civilized" European countries were engaged in this trade of human beings brought from African coasts to the Americas to be sold making huge profits out of it.

Their life was indeed hard. Slaves assigned to the mines and to the fields worked for fourteen, sixteen and even more hours daily; they were not allowed to rest, were only given a bite to eat and almost no clothes, not to mention the fact that they were denied an education. Sometimes a priest visited them, urging them to obey their masters and to resign to their fate, for it was God's wish that there be masters and slaves on earth. Some slaves were better treated than others, like the ones who worked in town or, when there was only one slave in a household, performed domestic chores or helped in some small crafts workshop; but slaves who worked in the big estates or in the mines were the victims of a brutal exploitation. Masters could savagely whip, shackle, lock up for days or put his slaves in the pillory to punish them. These and others were the tortures to break the slaves who failed to do their work to their master's satisfaction, or who rebelled and escaped, taking to the mountains or other hidden sites. Runaway slaves were called *cimarrones*, and the camps they set up to live as free men were called *palenques*. Several places throughout the island have borne the name "El Palenque" for a long time; this means that a group of runaway slaves probably lived there one hundred or more years ago.

Some say the slaves peacefully submitted to exploitation. That is entirely untrue. Since the first slaves arrived, many took to the mountains, sometimes together with the Indians, sometimes by themselves. Thousands of slaves in Cuba fought for four centuries against the *rancheadores* who, paid by slave owners, persecuted the runaways with their hounds and brutalized them. Endless abuse drove the slaves to desperation; they then resorted to self-inflicted wounds that would render them useless as miners or farmhands.

It is obvious that, after the Spaniards arrived in Cuba, a government and a society were established where a small group was rich and powerful, whereas the majority, although free, were dispossessed, while others were enslaved. Poor Spaniards and criollos usually owned small workshops where shoes were made or repaired; or bakeries or little retail shops; that is to say, they were engaged in countless urban economic activities. Some of them were hired as laborers. All this means that the exploited came from various backgrounds: they could be enslaved Africans, but they could also be salaried whites. It must not be forgotten that the exploitation of man by man has nothing to do with race or nationality, but is the consequence of the fact that some men wield power and own the land, the factories and the tools, whereas others—like the Indians, the African slaves and the poor whites—had nothing, except the strength to work.

How Cuban Wealth Was Plundered

The exploitation of the Indians and the Africans in the gold mines, in the production of casabe and in other economic activities by the conquistadors and the powerful has already been described. These men later engaged in selling leather to Spain and, therefore, breeding cattle became a must. There already were large farms—called *hatos* and *corrales*—where cattle was raised. The *monteros*—the men who tended the cattle—were either Indians or Africans who worked for the landowner. But it must be emphasized that many of those powerful, wealthy men were also interested in developing sugar cane plantations and in manufacturing sugar. They knew that to Europeans, sugar was an important foodstuff. European merchants were indeed interested in promoting the production of sugar in the Americas, for their traditional pre-Columbian suppliers—the Middle East, the north of Africa, Sicily and the Canary Islands—were unable to meet the growing consumers' needs. Soon, it became known that Cuba's soil and climate were perfectly suited to grow sugar cane, and many plantations were founded.

At first, sugar cane was consumed as a fruit, sucking it or squeezing the *guarapo* out of it by means of very simple implements. For example, the *cunyaya* squeezed out the guarapo from the cane to manufacture dark pan sugar loaves. Cunyayas have been found relatively recently in some remote areas in Cuba. But it was until 1590, almost one century after Diego Velázquez's arrival, that the first sugar mills were built. They were called *trapiches*, and its crushing wheels were moved either by mules, by oxen, or by African slaves. As a general rule, trapiches produced little sugar, for they did not squeeze enough guarapo from the sugar canes.

If we compare the machinery in modern sugar mills with a trapiche, we will realize the enormous differences between them. The trapiche predated the modern sugar mill by more than two hundred years, during which outstanding progress was made both in machinery and techniques to produce more and better quality sugar. These advances only benefitted sugar mill owners at that time. We have currently improved the machinery in sugar mills to produce sugar in more advantageous conditions for the workers.

The Spanish conquistadors also traded with tobacco grown in Cuba. They learnt the Indian way to grow it, for it was a crop exclusive of the Americas, unknown to Europe, Asia and Africa. The Spanish, the English, the French and the Dutch who came to the Americas as conquistadors took a liking to tobacco and made it known in their respective countries. Consequently, the tobacco trade flourished. Tobacco is a very delicate plant and, therefore, growers have to be very careful with it. In Cuba, peasants from the Canary Islands or born in the Americas cultivated it in small fields called *vegas*. The *vegueros*—the tobacco planters—usually had no slaves, for the small tobacco plantation was a family business. But they did not own the land and either leased it from the owner, or established their plantations in remote, ownerless places far away from town. Later on they had to fight the big landowners who wanted to expel them the land they cultivated.

As I said, sugar, cattle and tobacco were Cuban goods that were traded.

In Cuba, trade was always a major economic activity, but restrictions over goods for export determined a growing dependence in the country's international trade relations since the 16th century.

Since the conquistadors arrived in Cuba, several members of the oligarchy had been involved in selling goods produced on the island to merchants and speculators not only in Spain, but throughout Europe. It was precisely the trade carried out with Spain's colonies that sparked the struggle among European states over the control of the Americas.

Pirates, Privateers and Smugglers Appear

The Americas had just been discovered when the Europeans began to fight among themselves over its conquest and exploitation. The Spanish monarchs took advantage of their priority to create for themselves a vast and wealthy empire. Spanish traders and landowners also profited by these circumstances. These unleashed the ambitions of other European colonialists since the 16th century.

The Spanish colonial government, in order to protect Spanish interests, forbade traders from other countries to come to American and Cuban ports to barter their goods. That was how the colonial monopoly on trade operated. French, English and Dutch merchants also wanted to do business in the Americas and, prevented to do so by colonial Spanish laws, they sent pirate and privateer ships that approached Cuban shores, usually near sparsely inhabited places, contacted the people in the area, and bought tobacco, sugar and leather from them in exchange for European goods. When Europe had its own colonies in the Americas, trading with other countries was also forbidden, for all colonialists enforce similar policies everywhere.

It is true that some pirates attacked and pillaged towns and cities, but it must be remembered that there were almost no differences between merchants and pirates. Therefore, the struggle among Spanish and other European merchants and pirates was simply a conflict among people who exploited other men and plundered other countries' wealth. Their weapons were strength and cunning.

The Englishmen Francis Drake and Henry Morgan, and the Frenchman Francois Nau, known as l'Olonais, were among the most famous pirates of their time. There were also Spanish pirates. And even a Cuban mulatto, named Diego Grillo, became a pirate. Pirates and merchants respected no one. They looted or traded, according to circumstances, wherever they expected to obtain profits, and not caring whom they victimized with their excesses.

The Spanish government took measures against pirates and smugglers. It organized large men-of-war fleets, built fortresses, surveilled the coasts, threatened to punish anyone who contacted pirates and privateers, but to no avail: the authorities themselves, the governors, the clergy, city council members and landowners protected or were involved in that illegal commerce themselves. The measures taken by the Spanish government failed and smuggling continued to exist in Cuba for a long time.

Some times, pirates and privateers had special permission from their respective governments and they were even granted honorary titles. At other times, they appeared under the guise of big commercial enterprises that attacked Spanish fleets and colonies. At a given time, pirates and privateers had become so active, that it was quite dangerous to sail Cuban waters.

By the year 1650, the French, the English and the Dutch succeeded in taking over certain territories in the Americas. They settled permanently in the northern region of the continent (Canada and the United States), and in the Antilles.

The First Social Conflicts

As the exploitation of the considerable Cuban agricultural wealth began other, albeit few, immigrants arrived in the country. The island was only sparsely populated. Other territories in the Americas seemed to attract more settlers for, besides having large indigenous populations who were forced to work for the settlers, they also had plenty of gold and silver mines, coveted by oligarchies on both sides of the Atlantic. Furthermore, as those settlers showed no special interest in Cuba, the successive Spanish governments lost interest in its colony.

The small ruling groups in the various Cuban cities grew slowly; they were powerful because they were privileged. A few families owned most of the land. Thus, when trade with Spain expanded, these landowners became gradually interested in growing tobacco and other cash crops, and even put some of the land previously devoted to livestock, to that use. These changes brought about the first agrarian conflicts in the history of Cuba.

The vegueros—criollo peasants or peasants who came from Spain or from the Canary Islands looking for a small plot of land, mainly on the banks of a river to grow tobacco—have already been mentioned. Between the years 1600 and 1620, many of these peasants went deep into the Cuban country-side, looking for land. For instance, many of these vegueros settled near various rivers in the province of Havana, on the banks of the Cuyaguateje in Pinar del Río, along the Agabama, Caracucey and other rivers in the former province of Las Villas. Landowners soon realized that the land where tobacco and sugar cane were grown was much more productive than the one devoted to livestock, and they began to plot how to seize the vegueros' land or force them to pay rent. The landowners were members of the small group of exploiters who controlled the colony at the time and, protected by the power they wielded, purported to deprive the vegueros of their land. Logically, a struggle ensued, for the vegueros resisted the landowners' claims. We will delve further on into some aspects of this struggle, but at this point, it must be said that they fought against their enemies for more than two hundred years.

The most exploited groups were precisely the ones who began the struggle against injustice in Cuba. The first ones to rebel around the year 1528, were the Indians headed by the cacique Guamá. Later, came the struggle of the vegueros and of the African slaves brought to Cuba, who had always confronted their brutal exploiters. It is true that the slaves, due to the type of exploitation they suffered, were unable to organize large protest movements like the vegueros did but, as we have already mentioned, many slaves took up whatever weapons they could lay their hands on, fought against the rancheadores, and founded palenques on the mountains or in caves where no one dared to follow them. During four centuries, the masters' main concern was to prevent their slaves from having access to weapons or from coming together in large numbers, unless they met under the watchful eyes of an armed group of whites. The masters knew the slaves rejected the oppression to which they were submitted.

The Spanish monarchs sent numerous governors to Cuba during the first two centuries. They were generally replaced every five years. Diego Velázquez, the man who conquered the territory, was the first governor. Many were appointed after him, most of them only intent on becoming rich. Some carried out public works, specially fortresses to defend the colony against other European conquistadors. But others engaged in conflicts with the small group of men who owned anything of value on the island. However, they usually reached an agreement in the end.

Very few governors were cultured men; they were mostly military men appointed as governors to reward their participation in the European wars. One of them, called Juan de Tejeda, granted further momentum to ship building, a budding industry just before his arrival. Since then, until the early 19th century, rather large vessels were built in Cuba, mainly men-of-war made from hardwood that abounded on the island.

Occasional clashes and tensions took place among the higher colonial authorities (governors, commanders of the forts, bishops and city councilors). They were apparently sparked by trivial issues, but behind these incidents, there often lurked major economic and power-related motives. Several governors had to face the criollo—the Cuban-born offspring of Spaniards—oligarchy, and at times the "natives" or "habaneros" (the criollos) formed one faction, while the Spaniards formed another.

Catholic clergymen came to Cuba together with the conquistadors. There was at least one church in each city, and there were many more in Havana. A large number of bishops came and went, but left no traces of their stay in Cuba, having left nothing to remember them by. Usually, the Catholic clergy preferred to live in the cities, for the peasant population was very poor and less numerous, and therefore contributed little to the priests' sustenance. Many of these priests lacked the morals they were supposed to uphold, eliciting protests from bishops like Armendáriz and Diego de Compostela (1635-1704). Other priests and friars devoted themselves to teaching, for classes were imparted in the convents.

A barely developed colony, sparsely inhabited and lacking financial resources, Cuba's cultural life remained uneventful until the mid-18th century.

PART II

18TH CENTURY

Effects of Economic and Political Changes
in Europe
The Beginning of Neocolonization

...For it is an offense against His Majesty and against the fatherland to take up arms and avail of such means of defense only
permitted to kings...

CABILDO OF HAVANA[1]

1. Speech to tobacco growers who had risen up in arms against the
ban issued on the tobacco trade by colonial authorities; April 1717.

Major changes were taking place in Europe and in Spain in the 17th century. Thanks to commerce, England was on its way to becoming the strongest European power. Capitalism had sprouted strong roots in England since the 17th century. The country had a large merchant fleet and a mighty navy; it was also quite industrialized, specially in regard to textiles. France was also becoming a big power. Holland, in its turn, had succeeded in developing vast trading relations throughout the Americas and Asia. Spain and Portugal, that had wielded considerable power one hundred years before, were beginning to decline. Spain's merchant fleet and navy were dwindling.

The Spanish people suffered under the yoke of the landed gentry. A regionally-torn economy prevented industrial development and the organization of a national domestic market. The fact that the Catholic monarchs had expelled from the country or constantly hounded Spain's Arab and Jewish population worsened the situation. The former were mainly farmers and artisans; the latter were big, very wealthy merchants. Spain did not manufacture many of the goods in demand in its American colonies. Therefore, Spanish merchants were obliged to buy from other European countries, paying with the silver and the gold mined in the Americas for the textiles, metal goods and tools, jewels and many other products, which they sold in the Americas at high prices. Unlike England and France, Portugal and Spain—that restricted itself to trade—did not succeed in developing their economies.

Various aspirants to the throne appeared when King Charles II of Spain (1661-1700) died without a successor. France, England and other European powers went to war to decide by dint of force which of their respective candidates would be the next king of Spain. This happened around 1701. The war lasted several years and ended with the signing of a series of treaties in Utrecht, in the year 1713. A French prince was proclaimed King of Spain under the name Philip V (1683-1746). Barely fifteen years before, in 1697, the important Ryswick Peace Treaty had ended a long series of European wars. The violent struggle among the most developed European countries to rule over the Americas, Africa and also Asia, seemed endless. Pirates, privateers and other assailants would no longer attack Cuba. From then on, the attackers would be the European armadas, intent on seizing the island away from Spain. Piracy and aggression had become a part of the official policy enforced by the governments of the most developed capitalist countries. During the war that began in 1701, Cuba was threatened in several occasions by foreign fleets, and it also harbored French merchant and warships, for France and Spain were allies at that time.

The war brought about a strong current of mercantile and industrial speculation, which also had its effects on Cuba. Many new trapiches and mills to manufacture snuff—in great demand in Europe—were built. At the time, Europeans were not acquainted with cigars or cigarettes. The snuff manufactured in Cuba became quite famous. French and English ships that brought slaves to Cuba, loaded sugar, tobacco and untanned leather. This period of intense trade ended around 1720. From then on, the colonialist policy that prevailed was aimed at preventing Cuba from trading with other countries. A good many sugar and tobacco mills were dismantled or closed down. However, the island's fertile soil had begun to attract the attention of the European powers.

During the war, the Spanish government purported to control Cuban tobacco crops by means of a commercial monopoly. Various regulations were issued to force the peasants to sell their entire crops to the Spanish king's agents. This sparked a revolt by tobacco planters—the vegueros—, who had struggled against landlords for one hundred years. There were many tobacco plantations around Havana, some of them located in small towns like Jesús del Monte and San Miguel del Padrón that became a part of Havana as the city grew and engulfed them, and others in neighboring Santiago de las Vegas. Tobacco planters had chosen the sites for their plantations near Havana to facilitate the shipping of their produce to Spain; others established themselves in faraway places, like Guane, Sagua and Trinidad where, however, tobacco sold well, mainly to smugglers.

When the Spanish government decreed in 1717 that Cuban tobacco had to be mandatorily sold to the king's commercial agents, tobacco planters near Havana organized a strong protest movement. The king's agents indulged in all kinds of excesses, delayed payments, refused to buy parts of the crops, alleging low quality, and threatened not to make further purchases. The planters complained to the authorities in Havana, but not even the governor paid heed. Discontent grew and, on that same year, hundreds of tobacco planters, armed with picks, lances and farming tools, marched on Havana and surrounded the Castillo de la Fuerza, where the governor lived. The governor unsuccessfully tried to divide the movement to make it fail; after resisting the onslaught for a short time, he had no other choice but to flee for Spain. Repression ensued. But because the conditions in which the tobacco was purchased from the peasants remained unchanged, the discontented planters staged a new protest in 1721. The government was obliged to compromise, for the planters threatened with even stronger demonstrations. For a second time, the authorities promised not to pursue the rebels and offered to improve the system of purchase and payment; some landowners even had to condone the payment of rents over the land.

Discontent grew, for the planters' circumstances worsened under the purchasing system in force. The king's agents gave the planters receipts for the tobacco they bought, which the planters were only able to cash when money arrived from Spain. As the money never arrived on time, the planters were forced to sell the receipts to moneylenders, who paid much less than what they were really worth. It is well known that, before the triumph of the Revolution, profiteers also exploited the peasants, buying their coffee or their tobacco crops at very low prices. It was therefore logical that, in 1723, the planters refused to sell their tobacco under these conditions like in 1717, an armed group readied to take over Havana. The governor learned about their intentions and sent his troops against them. The peasants at large had no weapons and no military experience. When they clashed with the governor's troops in the outskirts of Havana, the peasants scattered and the skirmish ended with some casualties and fatalities on both sides. Eleven planters were captured and later hung in Jesús del Monte. These demonstrations meant that problems had already arisen that in years to come would lead to popular protests and armed struggle until the triumph of our Revolution.

Cuban Merchants Come on the Scene

As the population grew, so did production and trade. In Havana, a group of rich and ambitious merchants slowly took shape. They believed that, if they were authorized by the king of Spain, they could control the entire island's trade, after the fashion of the western European trading companies founded in the 17th century. In 1739, they appointed a merchant from Havana—Martín de Aróstegui—as their representative. Aróstegui went to Madrid to set up a trading company that would monopolize all imports to and exports from Cuba. One year later, the Real Compañía de Comercio de La Habana (the Royal Trading Company of Havana) was founded, that monopolized the colony's trade until 1762. Spanish and Havanan merchants associated to it made huge profits, for they charged very high prices for the goods they brought from Europe and for slaves, and bought Cuban goods at very low prices. Merchants in Havana, Santiago de Cuba and other cities complained about the exploitation they suffered at the hands of this alliance of Cuban and Spanish merchants. However, no measure was taken against their excesses, for they were supported by the Spanish government. The Real Compañía de Comercio was closed after the English fleet seized Havana city in 1762.

Discontent and Attacks from Abroad

A wave of repression by Spanish colonial authorities broke out after the uprisings staged by tobacco planters. The colony had begun to stir. Philip V, King of Spain, inaugurated a hardhanded policy to face the discontent evinced by the Spanish people and the people in the colonies. He began by virtually suppressing the most important functions of the Cabildos, so that governors felt free to run affairs in Cuba in whatever way was most convenient for the Spanish government. Garrisons mushroomed, and military chiefs appointed from then on submitted their troops to a stringent regime. Slowly, but surely, the criollos—even those from aristocratic families— were prevented from occupying key civilian or military posts.

The Spanish government had realized that the criollos, although they came from wealthy families of merchants or landowners—that is to say, from the class that exploited the peasants and the slaves—, felt they were different from the Spaniards. It needs to be understood that, although Cuban merchants and landowners exploited the poor and the slaves, in their turn, the king and the powerful Spanish ruling classes dominated everyone, including Cuban merchants and landowners. Many people complained at the time about this increasingly repressive policy, and some even wrote to the king explaining that an unbearably oppressive tyranny prevailed in Cuba. As the world's history shows, the powerful are seldom discontent about the same things that cause discontent among the dispossessed. The powerful wanted to profit from Cuba's trade with other countries, forbidden by the Spanish government. The dispossessed protested against the abuses committed by the powerful who lived in the colony and by authorities sent by the metropolitan government. Complaints, clashes and disagreements, like the ones that took place in Camagüey in 1728, were constant. These circumstances encouraged the projects against Cuba cherished by other European governments and trading sectors. Available documents which date back to those years show that, since the 17th century, the Dutch and the English believed their project to take Cuba and other colonies away from Spain could benefit from the discontent of wealthy criollos and of slaves. That was why, in 1741, during one of the many wars the waged in Europe, English troops landed in Guantánamo and tried to establish a beachhead there, in order to advance on Santiago de Cuba and found an English colony on the island. Apparently, the climate and the difficult terrain prevented them from succeeding in this endeavor, which they had entertained since the previous century.

In 1762, twenty years after they had landed in Guantánamo, and due to another war in Europe that pitted England against France and Spain, the English seized Havana. Wars were quite frequent in those years due to the fierce competition among French, English, Dutch and Spanish capitalists. The entire world—Europe, Asia, Africa and the Americas—was their battleground. Wars during the 18th century were waged mainly by three or four countries that purported to parcel out the colonies and to rule over Europe.

When the English attacked and seized Havana, they were simultaneously attacking French colonies in the Americas (Canada and Guadaloupe), as well as other Asian colonial territories in what is now India. The attack against and the seizing of Havana lasted almost two months. The city was well protected by a series of fortresses, and the resistance that the Castillo del Morro put up against the invaders weakened only when the assailants landed in Cojímar, a place near Havana, from where the Spanish troops, due to the incompetence of their military chiefs, swiftly withdrew. However, the militia—an armed corps made up mainly of peasants and people who lived in Guanabacoa and Havana—, led by a peoples' hero, the alderman of Guanabacoa's city council, José Antonio Gómez, better known as Pepe Antonio, firmly resisted the invaders' onslaught. This shows the difference between the colonial mercenary troops and the Cubans, for whereas the former did not fight, the latter tried to defend their land at any cost. Havana surrendered on August 12, 1762. A group of women wrote a letter to the king complaining about the incompetence of the Spanish military chiefs, and pointing out that whenever a criollo criticized colonial mismanagement, he was accused of being a rebel and an enemy of Spain. It must be borne in mind that all this happened in 1762, and that those who exploited and oppressed the people, harassed justly discontented Cubans with false accusations.

One year after Havana capitulated, the English government exchanged the territory it had conquered for other Spanish territories. It was then that the Spanish colonial government realized how important Cuba was. Havana was a key point in the sea route between Mexico and Spain. The Spanish government and ruling classes received the riches plundered from Mexico, specially silver, by way of Havana. If a foreign power succeeded in taking hold of the city and used it as its operational base, it would be able to prevent all trade. Furthermore, the government realized that Cuba possessed many untapped riches, and that it would be convenient to exploit them on behalf of Spain's ruling classes. Thus, besides enforcing a few economic reforms, Spain sent governors to Cuba who set the administration of the treasury aright, improved the courts of law and undertook the construction of the first major public works on the island.

PART III

1. 19TH CENTURY

Slavery-based Colonialism at its Height
(1790-1868)
Initial Definitions of a National Culture
Growth of the Sugar Industry
The First Conspiracies
Colonial Repression

Whether (King) Fernando wants it or not, whatever the opinion of his vassals on the island of Cuba may be, a revolution in that country is inevitable. The difference will only be the time andthe way.[1]

PRESBYTER FÉLIX VARELA

1. *El Habanero.* 1824.

I t was necessary to reform some of the old laws that restricted trade, in order to further exploit Cuba's riches. That was why, in 1765, Havana was authorized to trade with various Spanish ports and, in 1778, also with foreign—other than Spanish—ships.

In 1776, the British colonies in North America began their struggle for independence. Since then, ships from those colonies were allowed to anchor in the port of Havana, where they bought Cuban goods in exchange for flour, equipment and gadgets made of iron, as well as slaves. After their independence, those colonies proclaimed themselves the United States of America. Its trade relations with Cuba began to develop. The newly proclaimed nation was still weak: it had resorted to France and Spain's aid in order to conquer its independence, but in time, it became strong and began to plunder Cuba's riches. In less than one century, the United States became the chief market for certain Cuban products. Later on, some enterprising North Americans invested their capitals in Cuba and bought Cuban properties; they swiftly took hold over the land and exploited the people until the Revolution nationalized all American companies. The United States, a country that had waged its own war of independence, became an enemy of Cuba's independence.

Trade increased after 1765, and the demand for sugar from Europe and the United States—as well as from other parts of the world—grew, for Cuban sugar was very important to merchants and refineries. In order to sell more sugar, production had to be increased and, therefore, many Cuban landowners began to build new mills and to modernize the existing facilities. At the time, a big mill's sugar cane plantations ranged only from 5 to 15 caballerías (1 caballería=33 acres) and produced barely 1,000 boxes of sugar, each weighing 16 arrobas (1 arroba=11.5 kilograms). But the fact that those mills were small and their productivity was low, did not mean their owners earned no profits; on the contrary, their gains were considerable.

More labor force was needed to increase profits from sugar and, consequently, in 1789, the owners asked permission from the colonial authorities to bring as many African slaves into the island as they deemed necessary. Always seeking to increase their gains, sugar mill owners forced the slaves to produce more by imposing harder tasks on them, lengthening their daily working hours and their working week, locking them up in barracks and frequently punishing them.

Sugar mill owners and the ruling classes knew that the slaves wanted to be free, so they repressed them and kept them under a strict surveillance. In the period from 1790 to 1799, the enslaved Haitian people rebelled against its masters, the French colonists. The example set by the slaves, that brought about the Haitian Revolution, caused panic among the ruling groups in Cuba.

Countless slaves in various sugar mills and coffee plantations mutinied in Cuba during those years; as in previous times, the exploiters feared that the revolutionary example set by a people could be imitated by another. Thus, they increased their vigilance over and repression against the slaves, and tried to isolate Cuba from Haiti.

The First Reformers

During the late 18th century, the Spanish government appointed Don Luis de las Casas (1745-1800) as Cuba's governor. He implemented a policy that benefitted sugar mill and plantation owner; Don Luis himself became a sugar mill owner. This is an example of the way in which rulers protect the interests of the powerful. Such things were common in Cuba until the Revolution put an end to the exploiters' alliance.

In the late 18th century, sugar mill owners in Cuba had an intelligent leader who voiced their ideas and was inspired by their interests. His name was Francisco Arango y Parreño (1765-1837), who was in favor of making the slaves work more, but who also believed it was necessary to spread technical knowledge to produce more and better quality sugar, coffee and other agricultural produce. He favored a freer trade, particularly with the United States, and the passing of laws abolishing a series of economic bans and obstacles in regard to land tenure, cattle breeding and the monopoly over tobacco crops and sales. Also at that time, the distinguished physician doctor Tomás Romay (1764-1849) contributed in no small measure to improve the teaching of sciences. By applying for the first time a vaccine against smallpox, he eradicated that highly contagious and lethal disease from the country. And last, but not least, Father José Agustín Caballero (1762-1835) took upon himself the task of spreading new ideas; he opposed the decadent scholastic philosophy and the obsolete teaching methods imposed by the traditional authorities of the Catholic Church.

Besides Arango y Parreño's writings about production problems, and Tomás Romay's scientific works, other cultural activities began to develop in Cuba. The newspaper *El Papel Periódico de La Habana* (The Periodical of Havana) was published. The first public library was founded in the premises of the Economic Society Amigos del País, which counted many landowners among its members. Naturally, the newspaper as well as the library and the Society itself dealt mainly with issues in which the powerful—that is to say, the big landowners, the sugar cane and coffee planters and the merchants—were interested in. However, these efforts that promoted teaching, technique and culture, were indeed important: the increase in production and trade came hand in hand with the development of science and culture, in general terms.

At the time, not only sugar and coffee production rose in the area that surrounded Havana, but also elsewhere on the island. For example, new sugar mills were built in Matanzas and many coffee plantations thrived in the area of Artemisa and, particularly, in the region close to Santiago de Cuba: the Sierra Maestra and the Guantánamo mountainous area.

By then, the Cuban nationality had begun to express itself under the guise of opposed economic interests between the big Cuban landowners and the ruling classes in Spain. The Cuban nationality had begun to emerge, although it was still weak, incomplete and immature. It would be necessary to change the social structures in order to allow the existence of a strong, well-defined Cuban nationality, and one of the decisive steps in that direction took place in 1868, when the patriots who had taken up arms against colonial domination, freed their slaves.

The Revolutionary Struggle Begins

Revolution erupted in France in 1789; the Parisian revolutionary masses took the Bastille—that symbolized the power wielded by the feudal monarchy—by storm. The independence of the United States and the French Revolution sparked a worldwide popular movement of rebellion against the oppression and the abuses of the ruling classes. This also happened in Cuba. Not only slaves protested and rebelled against their masters, but also free men who realized that the policies implemented by the Spanish government were harmful to the Cuban people. The slaves turned against their masters to protest against the exploitation to which they were subjected but, at the same time, many free men protested against the government and the powerful in Spain, who plundered Cuba's riches. This has often happened in the course of history: the poor in every nation confront the rich, but sometimes the latter have had to fight against others, richer and more powerful than themselves, like foreign capitalists and merchants.

It must not be believed that, in those times, the rich and the slaves were the only two opposed sides. Various middle class and poor sections of the population were also exploited by the country's wealthy few, and were discontent. Since 1810, middle class people, owners of small estates, professionals and civil servants, had begun to speak about independence, to organize uprisings to throw the Spanish colonists out of the country. A free black man, José Aponte, conspired to promote a slave uprising for freedom. The colonial authorities discovered the plot, and Aponte was sentenced to death and executed in Havana, together with some of the men who shared his ideals, in the year 1812.

At the turn of the century, France sent its troops to Spain, with which it was at war. The Spanish people indignantly rose against the foreign interference, and heroically defended its rights from 1808 until 1812. The Spanish government was weakened by these circumstances and, as discontent in most Spanish colonies in the Americas was widespread, a great war of independence broke out. The priest Miguel Hidalgo (1753-1811) in Mexico; Simón Bolívar (1783-1830) in Venezuela; Francisco Santander (1792-1840) in Colombia; José de San Martín (1778-1850) in Argentina and Bernardo O'Higgins (1776-1842) in Chile, led great movements for independence to expel Spanish colonialists from the continent. A long, drawn-out struggle began that lasted until approximately 1823, and concluded with

47

the patriots' victory. The armed struggle spread throughout the continent, and the revolutionaries everywhere defeated Spanish colonialist troops. Many Cubans took part in the struggles under way in other Latin-American countries like Mexico, Venezuela and Colombia, thus showing the solidarity that has always existed among our peoples. Latin Americans in Cuba, in their turn, also worked for independence.

The big sugar and coffee planters, the most powerful class on the island, were reluctant to embark on a revolutionary endeavor that could harm their thriving businesses and leave them without slaves. Therefore, despite the many conspiracies and the solidarity of all Latin America, a revolution capable of overthrowing Spanish colonialism was not organized. The successive North-American governments were also opposed to Cuba's independence and preferred that the country continue to be a Spanish colony. However, the great liberator Simón Bolívar, aided by Venezuelan and Colombian revolutionaries, organized an invasion to free Cuba, which failed. The Mexican President Guadalupe Victoria (1786-1843) supported other such projects.

Some of the conspiracies organized in Cuba were very important. One of them, known as Soles y Rayos de Bolívar, and another, called Gran Legión del Águila Negra, were supported by various Latin-American countries. The conspirators published manifestos and organized revolutionary groups in many towns, but the conspiracies were discovered, and colonial authorities imposed severe sentences on their participants. The great poet José María Heredia (1803-1839) was one of the persons most committed to these projects. His works are the first expression of patriotic values in the Cuban culture.

The Spanish Government realized that Cuba was intent on following in the footsteps of its other colonies, and therefore reinforced its garrisons on the island and invested governors with greater powers, so that they could abort any uprising and suppress mere protests. An era of terror was inaugurated in 1825. The colonial government adopted further measures— that mainly benefitted the big landowners, the sugar and coffee planters, the cattle breeders and the merchants—, to prevent a revolution from taking place in Cuba. Arango y Parreño's reformist program was carried out. Sugar and coffee planters wanted more freedom to trade with other countries, particularly with the United States. The metropolitan government granted them that freedom, although not as broadly as the reformers wanted them to be. Those same owners wanted no legal obstacles for buying and selling land; the colonial government granted them their wish and passed laws that allowed them to freely dispose of their land. In some areas, like Güines, they also coveted the lands of the tobacco planters, whom they were able to deprive of their estates thanks to the new legislation. Thus, wealthy Cubans, who feared a revolution that would lead to independence, became even more adamant in their stance, bearing in mind that the colonial government protected their interests.

Efforts by wealthy Cubans to prevent a revolution helped colonial authorities to unleash an even harsher repression against the demonstrations of discontent by the free population on the island. The slaves suffered from further exploitation and repression. An illustrious Cuban, José Antonio Saco (1797-1879), was forced into exile by Governor Miguel Tacón (1775-1855), about whom discontented Cubans said he ruled the island "by stamping his heels". Besides repression against the people at large, there was also widespread corruption that thrived on the clandestine slave trade. In 1820, the Spanish government had promised the English government to stop the slave trade, but landowners, merchants, slave traders and many civil servants—including the authorities in Madrid and the monarchs themselves—had a tacit agreement to continue smuggling slaves into the island, and making profits from a trade which was closely watched and hindered by the English warships. The always cruel slave trade acquired an even more brutal nature when it became clandestine. Sometimes, a ship carrying human "merchandise" threw it overboard, to avoid being captured by an English man-of-war. José Antonio Saco, an outstanding reformer, was banished from Cuba for spreading his ideas contrary to this trade. Other Cubans shared his views but, nevertheless, few were in favor of putting an end to slavery at the time; not even Saco cherished this idea. This was due to the fact that the most powerful and cultured Cubans owned large slave crews and feared they would be ruined if their slaves were freed.

Like it always happens, the powerful did not want social changes, and refused to recognize the rights of the exploited. But in the end, the need for change prevails and the exploited conquer their rights through revolution. The abolition of slavery took place in Cuba as a consequence of the 1868-1878 revolution.

In the period from 1830 to 1850, the slaves were more abused than ever before. But they began to stir as they learned that in other countries in the Americas, slavery had already been abolished. Thus, around the year 1843, a large number of free blacks and mulattos, and numerous slaves from Havana and Matanzas began to publicly express certain discontent. Driven by fear, the governor, the military and the landowners organized a horrible massacre of slaves and free blacks and mulattos. This heinous crime was then and now called "the trial of La Escalera". The detainees were cruelly tortured until they said whatever the authorities wanted them to, and blamed one another of deeds they had not committed. Many were sentenced to death and executed; others died in jail due to brutality, and still others were sentenced to long prison terms. One of the men put to death was the poet Gabriel de la Concepción Valdés, known as *Plácido* (1809-1844).

The Spanish government used this movement led by slaves and free blacks and mulattos to instil fear into all whites, especially property owners. The colonialists profited from the desire for freedom of the black population to stress racial hatred and social segregation. To this day, imperialists pit men of different races against each other, to prevent them from uniting in a common drive for freedom.

As years passed, trade increased, more sugar was produced and more tobacco and coffee were exported. Most Cuban goods were sold to the United States, England and other countries. Spain bought little, but sold much. A struggle ensued among Spain, England and the United States to sell more of their own goods to Cuba. It was the usual struggle among capitalist countries to exploit other weaker countries. In their turn, Cuban landowners continued to thrive, buying better and more modern machinery for their sugar mills, in order to increase their earnings.

Improvements in the Sugar Industry

As sugar mills were mechanized, more and higher quality sugar was produced; therefore, sugar mill owners increased their profits. Mechanization was mainly introduced in Havana and Matanzas. Sugar mills elsewhere on the island were old-fashioned and yielded less sugar, which meant that landowners in the central and eastern regions of Cuba were neither as wealthy nor as powerful as those in Havana and Matanzas, causing a regional division of the landowning class. Modern machines and tools had to be handled by a work force with technical know-how; the slaves were unable to handle the new equipment. In the mid-19th century, slaves were illiterate and worked most of the day; thus, they could not manipulate the then modern machines. Eventually, machinery operators began to appear. Most of them were foreign, for sugar mill owners tried to replace their slaves with Indians from Yucatán and with indentured Chinese workers, massively brought to Cuba under a regime that barely differed from slavery.

Thus, one of the most important aspects of slavery became apparent. On the one hand, slaves were not fit to cope with a mechanized industry, but on the other, it was increasingly harder to get African slaves, for English and French settlers, who had scattered throughout Africa, preferred to exploit Africans in their native countries than to sell them to the Americas. All this made slave labor more costly; it was only natural that many Cubans began to realize the advantages of abolishing slavery and establishing salaried work. But slave owners were precisely the most powerful and cultured Cubans. Consequently, in their attempts to delay abolishing slavery, they also hampered economic development. This *always* happens with the ruling classes. One has only to look at how imperialists act nowadays. They speak about the need to put an end to poverty and ignorance in the world, but instead of taking measures to eradicate them, they send armies, spies, the so-called "Peace Corps," saboteurs, Green Berets and all sorts of criminals to preserve the status quo in colonial and neocolonial countries. In short, they do nothing to eradicate extreme poverty and ignorance but, on the contrary, they maintain them, emphasizing the need for a worldwide revolutionary process. It happened thus in Cuba more than one hundred years ago. The contradiction between slavery and the development of productive forces had to be resolved by the revolutionary struggle for independence that lasted from 1868 until 1878.

If the facts and episodes that shaped the emergence and decline of annexationism and of colonial reformism are analyzed, it will become clear that, on the one hand, the former was intimately linked to the colonial history of the United States (its participation in the capture of Havana in 1762), while the latter was reasserted by the unchecked process of relative stagnation and of political and social disturbances under way in Spain since the 16th century. Indeed, no consciously proud people can bear neither one nor the other.

The fact that the United States purchased a large portion of Cuba's sugar strengthened many Cuban landowners' notion that the island should become a part of that country. Wealthy planters in the southern United States, who owned countless slaves, also wanted to Cuba on their side, in order to strengthen slavery in their own country. Furthermore, even before the year 1820, several North-American politicians and rulers had cherished the idea of appropriating Cuba. This convergence of interests brought about an annexationist movement, whose aim was making Cuba a part of the United States.

Annexationist conspiracies were organized since 1848. The one headed by Narciso López (1798-1851), a general in the Spanish army, who landed in Cuba with two expeditions in the years 1850 and 1851, was of utmost importance. López was captured by the Spaniards, sentenced to death and executed in Havana.

Several Cubans, however, perceived it would not be right for Cuba to fall into North-American hands. José Antonio Saco, for example, waged an important battle against annexation. But many landowners favored annexation, for it would simultaneously vanquish Spanish colonial rule and guarantee their continuing ownership of slaves, because slavery still existed in the United States and they hoped to enjoy the rights to which their class aspired. It did not even cross their minds that annexation merely meant changing from a Spanish colony into a North-American colony. Other Cubans wanted independence and rejected Spanish colonialism and North-American annexationism alike. As production increased, so did the ranks of poor people and workers. The latter participated in some of the conspiracies that took place between 1850 and 1860. At the time, a typographer named Eduardo Facciolo (1829-1852) published three issues of the clandestine newspaper *La Voz del Pueblo Cubano* (The Voice of the Cuban People), a feat which cost him his life. He was executed in Havana.

The situation on the island was quite tense. Slave owners realized that annexationist armed expeditions—like the one headed by Narciso López—could spark a slave uprising, and deemed it more convenient to attain their goals by peaceful means. Previously flourishing businesses began to decline: the price of sugar plummeted and bankruptcies ensued. Cuba strongly felt the consequences of its growing links with the world economy. It was in those years that a bloody civil war began in the United States, pitting the southern slave owners against the northern capitalists. Many North Americans, among them President Abraham Lincoln (1809-1865) himself, believed in the need to abolish slavery. The war lasted five years and, in 1865, slavery was finally abolished in the United States. This change of circumstances made numerous Cuban landowners and members of the wealthy classes abandon the idea of relinquishing the country to the United States, and organized a new political reformist movement. Cuban slave owners no longer wanted Cuba to be a part of the United States, for they had realized they would be forced to abolish slavery, but they also understood that, sooner or later, the slaves on the island would have to be freed. They did not want this to happen suddenly, but step by step and, therefore, the movement demanded that the Spanish government implement in Cuba a series of measures that benefitted the landowners and allowed slavery to be gradually abolished.

The Failure of Reformism

Reformers carried out huge campaigns in their newspaper *El Siglo* (The Century), and were summoned by the Spanish government to Madrid, in order to discuss the reforms needed in Cuba and in Puerto Rico, which was also a Spanish colony. But reforms harmed the interests some dominant groups in Spain, who opposed them. In the end, the Spanish government mocked the reformers not only by not even considering the measures they proposed, but also by fixing further taxes that harmed the interests of Cuban landowners. That was one of the causes of the first war of independence in Cuba.

Like it always happens, the powerful classes who demand reforms try to prevent revolutionary solutions; they ascertain that a peaceful solution is better. However, reformism has never yielded good results. Even today, there are people in various countries who say that poverty and exploitation can be gradually eliminated without resorting to a revolution, which is the only means to attain an adequate development, in order to meet the masses' needs.

In the 19th century, mainly in the central and eastern regions, some Cuban landowners also had small sugar mills and a few slaves. The decline in business and the new taxes levied by the Spanish government did them great harm. Save the landowners in Camagüey, the rest had not been sympathetic toward annexationism for, unlike those in Havana, they had virtually no direct links with the United States. They had not been enthusiastic reformers, either. Political movements in those areas had never been as strong as the ones in Havana and Matanzas. Landowners there were part of the old criollo population, whose sentiments about freedom had been taking shape for centuries: the idea of independence had grown strong in them.

Cultural Development

Since the late 18th century, culture had evinced an increasing vitality. As the great crisis of colonialism approached, cultural manifestations had acquired special traits based on reciprocal service and usefulness, and had become clearly militant. Numerous magazines and newspapers in Havana, Matanzas, Santiago de Cuba and other cities informed their readers and at the same time, were used by the writers as a means of communication. Their lives were generally ephemeral, but some of them, like *El Americano Libre* (The Free American), *El Revisor Político Literario* (The Political and Literary Review), *La Cartera Cubana* (The Cuban Portfolio), the *Revista Bimestre Cubana* (Cuban Bi-monthly Review), *El Plantel* (The School) and *La Moda* (Fashions), were extremely valuable.

Literature progressively acquired a national sense, and knew moments of greatness in the works by Heredia—whom we have already mentioned—, Domingo del Monte (104-1853), José Jacinto Milanés (1814-1863) and Cirilo Villaverde (1812-1894), an extraordinarily forceful narrator, who penned the novel *Cecilia Valdés*. By the mid-19th century, poetry blossomed, nurtured by Joaquín Lorenzo Luaces (1826-1867), Juan Clemente Zenea (1832-1871) and Rafael María Mendive (1821-1886).

There were also outstanding historians: José Antonio Saco published his great *Historia de la esclavitud* (The History of Slavery) abroad, while Jacobo de la Pezuela (1811-1882) and Pedro José Guiteras (1814-1890) published histories about the colonial period, still useful nowadays.

Félix Varela (1787-1853) was the main reformer in regard to philosophy. He was a thinker ahead of his time, a fervent defender of independence and an advocate of the abolition of slavery in 1823. His disciple José de la Luz y Caballero (1800-1862) was the most important teacher of his time, and imparted classes in his own school, El Salvador. In 1852, the University of Havana underwent a reform for, having been under the directorship of Dominican priests since 1728, it had failed to meet the most urgent needs posed by modernization.

Cultural life was indeed active, as proven by certain public debates about the Cuban—instead of Spanish—character of literature, and the long polemic about Cousin's philosophy. But most writers and men of science suffered from the effects of press censorship, of harassment or, even worse, of persecutions that forced them to go into exile for long spans of time and even for life.

Toward the 1850s, European cultural influence began to fade away under the drive of development in the United States whose propaganda, since then, began to shape the illusions of the more cultured sections of the population. However, there would come a time, after 1868, in which Cubans would begin to pass critical judgements about that country's social and political evolution.

PART IV

2. 19TH CENTURY

The Struggle for Independence
The 1868-1878 Revolution
The 1895 Revolution
Imperialist Intervention (1898-1902)

Cuba wants to be a great, civilized nation, to lend a friendly
hand and a fraternal heart to all other peoples.[1]

CARLOS MANUEL DE CÉSPEDES

...I am now at risk of giving my life for my country's sake as is
my duty, for it is thus that I understand it, and I am willing to
timely prevent, with Cuba's independence,
the United States from spreading across the Antilles and
pouncing, with that added strength, on our America. Whatever I
did to date, and will do in the future, is to that aim.[2]

JOSÉ MARTÍ

1. Manifesto of the Revolutionary Junta of the Island of Cuba,
Manzanillo, October 10, 1868.

2. *Letter to Manuel Mercado*, military camp at Dos Ríos, May 18, 1895.
This letter remained unfinished, for José Martí was killed in combat
on the following day.

When José Antonio Saco publicly opposed annexationist projects, he said that, if Cuba became a part of the United States, Cubans would lose their sense of nationhood, their essence as a people, for another language was spoken in the United States, whose mores and interests were different. Saco would rather continue to be a Spanish subject, albeit under a reformed colonial system. He was right to reject annexation, despite the fact that he himself represented an incomplete and weak Cuban nation, for the Cuban people was still deeply divided, due to the existence of hundreds of thousands of slaves.

It is said that a people becomes a nation when a series of factors that unite all the inhabitants of a country exist, granting that people certain characteristics that both identify and differentiate it from other peoples and nations. Those factors developed slowly in Cuba since the late 18th century (1760-1799)—and even before that—, and were still weak by the mid-19th century (1850-1860). However, many Cuban-born people wanted to be Cubans instead of being North Americans or Spaniards. Those who thought thus were the bearers of a stronger national sentiment than Saco and other of his contemporaries. It was precisely them who wanted to be Cubans first and foremost, the ones who, after the failure of reformism and the disaster of the great 1857-1866 economic crisis, took up arms and began fighting for independence.

National feelings continued to grow despite difficulties and discrepancies about other existing trends.

After the movement for reforms failed in 1866, a large number of Cubans from Oriente, Camagüey and Las Villas organized a conspiracy to fight for independence. Among them were Carlos Manuel de Céspedes (1819-1874), Francisco Vicente Aguilera (1821-1877), Pedro Figueredo (1819-1870), Donato Mármol, the Dominican Luis Marcano, and others. Landowners in Havana refused to help them because they feared losing their wealth, but those in Oriente continued to prepare for war. The revolutionary situation in the area of Manzanillo and Bayamo became progressively stronger. Carlos Manuel de Céspedes believed the struggle should begin at once, although the men willing to fight and the weapons they had were still insufficient; whereas others deemed it necessary to devote more time to preparations. By October, 1868, the Spanish authorities had learned about the conspiracy and decided to arrest everyone involved in it. To avoid being detained, Carlos Manuel de Céspedes decided to rise against the Spanish colonial rule and, on October 10 of that same year, issued the cry of independence or death in his sugar mill La Demajagua, near Manzanillo. Many were the heroic deeds carried out by the combatants for freedom who began the struggle. The revolutionaries clashed with the colonial troops and succeeded in taking over the city of Bayamo, where they established the first Revolutionary Government-in-Arms. Late in 1868, and early in 1869, groups of patriots in Camagüey and Las Villas launched their first military actions. Since the struggle began, the great military leader Ignacio Agramonte (1841-1873) stood out in Camagüey, as did Eduardo Machado in Las Villas.

The patriots attained major victories since their first encounters with the enemy and, therefore, they decided to meet in the town of Guáimaro to set up a single government and draft democratic laws for the revolution. The revolutionary Assembly at Guáimaro elected Carlos Manuel de Céspedes as the President of the Republic of Cuba, and approved a Constitution on April 10, 1869. From that time on, the revolution began to develop swiftly. Hundreds of patriots joined the liberation army. Apart from discontent landowners, the poor in the cities and the countryside, and slaves freed by the revolutionary forces swelled the ranks of the combatants for freedom. Many came from the underprivileged classes, like Antonio Maceo (1845-1896) and his brother José, Guillermo Moncada (1838-1895), Máximo Gómez (1836-1905) and others, and became great military chiefs in the heat of the struggle. Military chiefs like Ignacio Agramonte, who always stood out for his personal courage and his organizing abilities, also emerged elsewhere in the country.

In a "popular" sense of the term, it was possibly in the eastern region where people considered as marginals or discriminated against had a more active participation in the slow formation of a *Cuban* civil society.

But perhaps due to that same reason—although this is not easy to clarify—two or three contradictory trends took shape among the traditional oligarchic groups. One of them advocated for total independence, while another favored a reformist colonial agreement among regional leaders or chieftaincies. Among the partisans of the former trend, organizing the war was a major issue, as was allowing younger people to join in the struggle, like it happened in 1869 in José Martí's case, who was barely 15 years old then. Those contradictions did not go unnoticed by colonial authorities, who based on them a policy aimed at eroding the revolution and weakening the combatant forces. This led to the Zanjón Treaty, signed in 1878, which paved the way to a second, equally opportunistic, colonial reformist trend.

Disagreements emerged among Cuban revolutionaries, for not all of them saw eye to eye in regard as to how the revolution should be conducted. Some revolutionary leaders thought military chiefs should be granted unchecked freedom of action, whereas others thought the military should be subordinated to the Chamber of Representatives. Some wanted to grant more power to Carlos Manuel de Céspedes, and others to the Chamber of Representatives. But these disagreements did not prevent the development of the revolution, because Cubans hated Spanish colonialism. The revolutionary might of the Cuban people was indeed powerful in the provinces of Oriente, Camagüey and Las Villas. Numerous guerrilla encounters and military actions involving thousands of men from both contending sides, were so many victories for the revolutionary forces.

The revolution gained no such strength in Matanzas, Havana and Pinar del Río, for the great land and slave owners supported the Spanish colonial power. This does not mean, however, that there were no patriots in the capital city: some of them joined the Liberation Army, while others carried out pro-independence propaganda or helped the Cuban troops. Early in 1859, several clashes took place with colonialists in Havana, in which José Martí (1853-1895) participated and was sentenced to forced labor for it. The idea took shape of invading the country's western region to include it in the struggle. The plan was to have a great revolutionary army march from Oriente across Camagüey and Las Villas, and spread into Matanzas and Havana, where the largest Cuban sugar mills were located. If they succeeded in doing this, the revolutionaries would be able to make a huge mass of slaves take up arms. An invading army was formed during the years 1873 and 1874, under the command of General Máximo Gómez. In Camagüey, Gómez and his troops waged major battles— like La Sacra, Palo Seco, Los Naranjos and Las Guásimas— against the Spanish colonial army. A vanguard column of the said invading army reached very near Colón city, but the invasion did not continue its thrust for lack of men and weapons. This, however, did not diminish the courageous struggle in Oriente and Camagüey throughout the year 1875, led by military chiefs like Antonio Maceo, Serafín Sánchez, Máximo Gómez and other patriots.

The Spanish government realized it was unable to vanquish the revolutionaries, and bid its time with promises of a peaceful settlement. Contradictions among the revolutionary leaders became more acute, facilitating the Spanish government's divisive maneuvers. The president of the Republic-in-arms was changed several times. In 1874, Carlos Manuel de Céspedes was deposed, and later fell in combat. The Chamber also relieved Céspedes replacement of his post. Tomás Estrada Palma (1835-1908), another of these presidents, was arrested. Calixto García (1839-1898), one of the great military chiefs in Cuba's eastern region, was captured by the enemy in 1874, severely wounded after trying to commit suicide. All these developments coincided in time, partially weakening the revolutionary leadership.

The colonialist maneuvers yielded fruit. On February 10, 1878, a group of revolutionary chiefs, in agreement with Spanish military authorities, signed the Zanjón Treaty, that promised limited reforms to the Cuban people. But none of the basic demands that had sparked the ten-year long war had been met. Not all the chiefs—and much less the soldiers—of the revolutionary army accepted that Treaty. A large number of patriots, like generals Antonio Maceo, Goyo Benítez, Ramón Bonachea and others continued to fight. Maceo ascertained that Spanish colonialists had satisfied none of the Cuban demands, and were only requesting that the patriots accept the peace and lay down their arms. He also believed they had to force the Spanish government to abolish slavery, for there were still hundreds of thousands of slaves on the island. Antonio Maceo and other patriots opposed the Zanjón Treaty by means of the Baraguá Protest. Months later, Maceo decided to go abroad to rally the support of Cuban émigrés, but to no avail. He stayed abroad, for it was impossible to continue fighting, but maintained that the war must go on.

It did in 1879, and revolutionary chiefs like Calixto García, José Maceo, Guillermón Moncada and Quintín Banderas (1834-1906) participated in it, in cooperation with José Martí. The fact that many of the military chiefs and soldiers were disappointed, prevented this new insurrection—known as the Little War—from developing further. The new movement's chiefs, and José Martí himself, deemed it was not possible to continue the struggle successfully and, in 1880, the uprising ended.

The death of its more determined members and its economic ruin had virtually eliminated the radical wing of the Cuban landowner class, by the time when the 1868 revolutionary movement came to an end. No other group of revolutionary landowners like the one that led the 1868 uprising came together in Cuba again. On the contrary, the landowner class became colonialist, reactionary or annexationist; in short, it became conservative.

It is highly probable that a new class formation emerged during the war, that had weakened slavery considerably. Consequently, traditional landowners began to show the traits of future capitalist businessmen, whereas the slaves, who had become salaried workers, were meant to strengthen the future proletariat, capable of maturing and perfecting the nation.

New Class Formations

The 1868 Revolution accelerated the process aimed at abolishing slavery. Since the mid-19th century, the country debated what would the future of the Cuban society be, due to the technological transformations of the sugar industry, the rise in the price of slaves smuggled into the island in violation of international agreements, and the development of a social consciousness that did not respond to the interests of the big slave owners. Colonialist policies that flaunted the "danger" of slave uprisings subsided, due to the appearance of national feelings. Many revolutionary slave owners freed their slaves, and the government of the Republic-in-arms approved laws and decrees that shaped the abolitionist policy. A large number of Cubans of African descent fought in the wars of independence, showing extraordinary qualities. Martí ascertained that the brotherhood among all Cubans was forged by the common struggle and ideals upheld by the 1868 revolution.

After the war ended, the colonial government was obliged to abolish slavery, which it did between 1880 and 1886. Thus began the most important process of social transformation to take place after four hundred years of colonialism. Why was the abolition of slavery such a decisive step? Because all workers became equal; from then on, they were proletarians. This means that the abolition of slavery marked the beginning of the formation of the working class.

Like the war, that had ruined an important section of the old landowner class that had participated in the struggle, the development of the sugar industry, based on costly sugar mills, also contributed to that class's demise. Sugar planters who were also slave owners, disappeared: some of them became bourgeois industrialists; others—who would later be known as *colonos*—lost their mills and became capitalist landowners devoted to growing sugar cane. In short, social classes and groups condensed in the two classes typical of capitalism: the bourgeoisie and the proletariat. Between these two extremes, a then increasingly impoverished middle class or petit-bourgeoisie existed.

Martí was aware of the political role of white, mulatto, black, Spanish and Cuban workers in deciding Cuba's fate; therefore, it is easy to understand the importance of the abolition of slavery and the establishment of a society with more clearly defined classes. Martí realized that the working class would embody the loftiest patriotic feelings.

Reformists Appear Again

After the two wars, began a new stage in the history of Cuba. Successive Spanish governments failed to fulfill the promises made to Cuban revolutionaries, contained in the Zanjón Treaty. The Goverment did not make significant reforms.

Colonialists continued to plunder Cuba's riches and the police and the army continued to harass discontent Cubans. Some Cuban landowners and petit-bourgeois founded the so-called Liberal or Autonomist Party, that contended with the Constitutional Union—the most reactionary party at the time—during elections. These elections were held to choose the members of each party that would represent Cuba at the Chamber of Representatives and the Senate in Madrid. Most Spanish representatives and senators were associated to powerful groups opposed to changing the way in which Spain ruled Cuba. The few Cuban representatives in Madrid were bound for failure; their hands were tied, even if they really wanted to improve their country's circumstances.

The liberals or autonomists convened meetings in Havana and in a provincial town where speeches were delivered to expose the colonialist government's deception. Many partisans of independence attended those meetings and supported the criticisms which, nevertheless, never materialized in any consistent political action, for autonomists were true to their criteria about reforms and peaceful struggle which, in the end, yielded no adequate results. In fact such criticisms were meant to deceive the people. Needless to say that most participants in the 10-year long war were in exile, and those who remained in Cuba had distanced themselves from reformist political action and kept the memories of that heroic war alive. Despite political persecution, some liberators—like Manuel Sanguily (1848-1925) and Juan Gualberto Gómez (1854-1933)—wrote books and booklets where they openly stated the need to fight for Cuba's independence. The autonomists' failure paved the way to those who advocated independence.

Could something positive have resulted from reformism? They proclaimed peace in Cuba, but the colonial government continued to repress the Cuban people. Their peace only made it easier for colonialist exploiters to enjoy their privileges and perks. That is also happening nowadays in various parts of the world; while they proclaim that social peace leads to development and well-being, imperialists continue to plunder the natural resources of the countries under their yoke; extreme poverty, illiteracy and unemployment increase, while progressive and revolutionary people are savagely persecuted.

The New Revolutionary Movement

The movement for independence experienced a new rise since 1887. It had a leader, a brilliant, unselfish man who devoted himself to it: José Martí, whose political activity from 1869 on is well known. He was barely sixteen years old on that year, when he was sentenced to forced labor.

Exiled since 1871, Martí lived in Spain and made extensive travels in Latin America, getting acquainted with its problems and taking part in progressive movements in various countries; he kept abreast of developments in his own country, like the abominable execution of eight medical students. He settled in the United States in 1880. There, he realized that that nation's big economic interests, the monopolies' executives, the rulers and the politicians associated to those interests, had their eyes on Cuba and on all Latin America, seeking to profit from their riches. He understood the negative sign of education for profit and violence that prevailed in that country. Martí confronted the then nascent imperialism and pointed out its aggressive nature; he denounced the economic character of its domination, and laid the groundwork for a common Latin-American stance. He was the first active thinker and fighter in our continent, who consciously devoted his life to prevent North- American financial capitalism from appropriating other peoples' riches and exploiting their work force. That is why it can be said that his work as a revolutionary organizer, and the new war or liberation that began in 1895, coincided with the study of those times carried out by the great Vladimir Ilich Lenin (1870-1924) who, thirty years later, analyzed the phenomenon of imperialism with unparalleled profoundness.

Martí understood the importance of the country's impoverished working masses. He took it upon himself to raise the consciousness and organize the thousands of Cuban workers who had emigrated to the United States, where many of the participants in the 10-year long war had also settled. Martí's greatest efforts were directed at uniting the impoverished people with the liberators of the 1868-1878 war so that, together, they would be the main force of the future revolution. In order to unite the people and organize the revolution, he founded the Cuban Revolutionary Party in 1892, whose aim was to fight for Cuba's independence. Like Simón Bolívar and other great men in American history, José Martí understood that Latin-American solidarity was necessary for the struggle, and he decided to fight for the independence of Puerto Rico as well, requesting the support of the peoples of the entire continent. The Cuban Revolutionary Party published *Patria* (Fatherland), a newspaper where the aims of the Cuban revolution were defined, and the ideals of independence were praised. Besides being a great organizer and political leader, Martí was also a shrewd thinker, who conceived a radical, popular bourgeois democracy; he was also an extraordinary poet, one of the Spanish-speaking pioneers of modernism. His activities were always centered on issues that affected the society of his time, and his pained fatherland. Years after his death, his *Obras completas* (Complete Works) were collected in 28 volumes.

The bulk of exiled Cuban workers in the United States supported Martí's program of action. Many of them gave part of their meager salaries to buy arms for the future revolution. The 1868-1878 liberators also rallied around the Cuban Revolutionary Party and Martí's program. The propaganda carried out abroad reached Cuba, and many old soldiers, together with the younger generation of revolutionaries, began to organize groups to take up arms whenever the Cuban Revolutionary Party ordered them to do so. The uprising was prepared in close coordination with Máximo Gómez and Antonio Maceo, and took place on February 24, 1895.

The landowners did not join the revolution; the liberation forces were made up mainly of urban, popular and rural petit-bourgeois. The autonomists continued to speak about reforms and therefore, became sworn enemies of the revolution and unconditional allies of Spanish colonialism.

The uprising took place simultaneously in various regions, like Oriente and Matanzas. A few days later, numerous patriots engaged in the first combats with colonial troops. Antonio Maceo landed on the northern coast of Oriente, and joined the liberation army. Together with Máximo Gómez, Martí landed in Playitas, in the southern coast of Oriente. The enthusiasm among the rank and file when they learned that their best loved and most experienced leaders were in Cuba, was a decisive factor. Thousands of men and numerous women joined the struggle, as did many young people 14 to 20 years of age, in response to the Cuban Revolutionary Party's appeal for independence.

The leaders of the revolution met at the La Mejorana estate to decide how to organize the government and the army. The Cuban Revolution acknowledged Máximo Gómez and Antonio Maceo—appointed General-in-Chief and Lieutenant General of the Liberation Army, respectively—as the military leaders. Martí, who planned to rally Latin-America's support for the revolution that would liberate Cuba and Puerto Rico, was scheduled to travel abroad. But he, who was the chief exponent of Cuban patriotism, was killed during the combat of Dos Ríos, on May 19, 1895, a few days after that meeting. However, the revolution did not ground to a halt: its leaders agreed to spread the war throughout the island, which meant carrying out the invasion frustrated in 1873-1874. To this end, a contingent was formed that would fight in all of the island's departments. This extraordinary military feat, known as the east to west invasion, was led by Máximo Gómez and Antonio Maceo. They departed from the place known as Mangos de Baraguá where, in 1878, Maceo had protested against the Zanjón Treaty. They overcame the colonial army in a series of major battles. As they advanced toward the island's western region, more and more combatants joined them. The bulk of the Cuban troops was still fighting in their own provinces and areas, and others joined the invading army. (During the revolution led by Commander-in-Chief Fidel Castro, two invading columns were also organized, under commanders Ernesto Che Guevara (1928-1967) and Camilo Cienfuegos (1932-1959), that advanced across Camagüey to Las Villas, where they seized the city of Santa Clara and several other towns, thus effectively destroying Batista's dictatorship.)

The invading column, under Gómez and Maceo's command, reached Havana on January 1, 1896. The liberation forces waged and won several battles on that province's reduced territory, where Spain had concentrated most of its troops. Gómez and Maceo parted in Havana. Gómez remained there, harassing the enemy, while Maceo led the rest of the invading column to Pinar del Río, Cuba's westernmost province. Maceo ended the invasion at Mantua, a town in Pinar del Río which he reached on March 22, 1896. The intended results had been attained: the war of liberation was being waged throughout the island. Once he had finished that immortal campaign, the Bronze Titan returned to Havana, where he was reunited with Gómez. They fought together at Moralitos and continued their heroic struggle in Havana and, later on, in Matanzas. There they said farewell—this time forever—at the Galeón encampment, near the town of Bolondrón. Maceo again marched toward the west, waging daily battles. After an intense campaign in Pinar del Río, he began the long march supposed to take him back to Oriente province. Together with a little group of combatants he crossed the Mariel bay by sea, and entered the Punta Brava area in Havana, where he contacted Cuban forces fighting there. His small camp was attacked by surprise by a Spanish column. Maceo, after recovering from the surprise, rallied his troops and was preparing to counterattack, when he fell mortally wounded by Spanish bullets. It was December 7, 1896. His death was a very hard blow for the revolution, not only because it lost a great combatant, but also a man of profound feelings and firm political principles.

Despite this blow, the revolution did not falter. A Government Council was organized, chaired by Salvador Cisneros Betancourt (1828-1914); a new constitution, as well as new laws to bring to life a revolutionary state, were drafted. In his capacity as General-in-Chief, Máximo Gómez guided the organization and activity of the entire liberation army from his headquarters in Las Villas. In Oriente, Calixto García had replaced Maceo as regional military chief. Many other leaders were active in the remaining provinces; their names alone would make a long list.

There were violent clashes between the patriotic forces and colonialist troops. But the Spanish leaders, furious because of their inability to defeat the liberators, appointed Valeriano Weyler (1838-1930) as Governor and Captain General of Cuba. Weyler implemented several brutal measures against the rural population. He issued an edict on concentration, forcing the peasants to live in cities and towns protected by colonialist garrisons. (This criminal system was also used and developed by the United States Army in South Viet Nam. Is it not the concentration decreed by Weyler a clear precedent of the "strategic villages" created by North-American imperialists in Viet Nam? Both are similar crimes.) That mass of peasants concentrated in towns and cities could not find work, food or lodgings, because the land ceased to be tilled and production was paralyzed in almost the entire country. It is estimated that 300,000 people died as a consequence of the famine policy implemented by Weyler. But colonialists also failed to defeat the Cuban liberators with this criminal measure. It can be said that all the Cuban countryside was in the hands of the revolutionaries, and only towns and cities under strict Spanish protection were able to resist the onslaught of the Cuban forces. Each passing day was further proof that the colonialists were doomed to failure in Cuba.

Although the liberators were strong, they lacked the decisive elements with which to definitively crush the colonialists. For example, they lacked artillery, cannons able to destroy Spanish fortresses. The huge efforts made by Cuban émigrés to collect money and send expeditions with weapons and men, were not always successful. Unscrupulous North-American traders sold outdated arms and ships to the Cuban revolutionaries, at very high prices; they later warned United States authorities about the expeditions. Thus, the cargo was confiscated and the expeditionaries arrested or scattered. The imperialist government of the United States put in practice a hypocritical policy of feigning sympathy for the Cubans, but at the same time serving Spanish colonialist interests, thus making it difficult for expeditions to leave for Cuba.

The Spanish colonialist government admitted in 1897 that Weyler's measures had not yielded the expected results. The liberators, on the other hand, had begun to burn down the main centers of the colonialist economy. The country was in ruins, and a worldwide campaign against the Spanish government's criminal policy in Cuba was launched. Some Spanish groups and political parties believed that the time had come to demagogically maneuver to destroy the revolution, for discontent had increased in Spain over a war that was taking its toll on the people. Therefore, it was decided to introduce changes in the way Spanish authorities ruled in Cuba, as of January 1, 1898. According to that decision, the Spanish governor would be aided by five secretaries from the Liberal (Autonomist) Party. By appointing these secretaries, Spanish colonialist leaders tried to deceive the people, weaken the revolution and pretend that the country would be ruled by its nationals. As this autonomous government was established, Spain sent emissaries to the Cuban leaders in order to convince them to lay down their arms, to no avail, for most chiefs and soldiers of the Liberation Army remained loyal to the patriotic ideal of independence.

Imperialist Ambitions Are Exposed

While feelings of solidarity for the Cuban people grew among North Americans, politicians and big economic interests in the United States believed the moment had come to intervene in the war between the Cuban people and the Spanish colonialists. Their feelings were quite different to that of the North-American people, they were not interested in making justice, imperialists were only concerned about seizing our country to exploit its natural resources. A North American man-of-war, the battleship *Maine*, was sent to Havana. It was anchored in the bay when it blew up on February 15, 1898. North-American propaganda accused Spain of causing the explosion, although it was later found out that was not true. If Spanish authorities in Cuba had not sabotaged the ship, only North-American warmongers could be blamed for the incident, that served as a pretext to declare war on Spain. North-American imperialism took advantage of this and other incidents to rouse more ill feelings among the contending parties.

On March, 1898, North-American politicians and the government of President William MacKinley (1843-1901) were ready for war and, without any previous declaration, they began military operations in April. On April 18, the North American Congress passed a resolution, stating that Cuba was, and by law should be free and independent. Other paragraphs in that same resolution contradicted this assertion, and showed that imperialists were not interfering in the war between Cuba and Spain to turn over the island's government to the liberators, but to remain in the country as its masters.

During the Spanish-Cuban-North American war, the United States requested the aid of the Cuban liberators, but did not recognize the Cuban Revolutionary Party or its Delegation in New York; neither did it recognize the Government Council chaired by General Bartolomé Masó (1830-1904), nor the General-in-Chief of the Cuban army. If imperialists had interfered in the war to contribute to Cuba's independence, they would have recognized both the revolutionary government and the leadership of the Liberation Army. President MacKinley's government directly requested Calixto García's help. The great

Cuban military chief not only advised North-American military chiefs about their military plan, but also backed the landing of North-American troops and the assault on Santiago de Cuba with Cuban forces. Without the decisive aid of the Cuban troops, the North-American soldiers would not have been able to land successfully, nor would they have defeated the Spanish army in such a short time.

The war's final campaign was characterized by the brilliant actions carried out by the Liberation Army under Calixto García's command. The chiefs of the Spanish colonialist army, cut off from reinforcements, surrendered to the North-American forces after the battles at El Caney and San Juan. The North-American military chief, General Shafter, hypocritically prevented the Cuban forces from coming into Santiago de Cuba. This behavior prompted Calixto García, who withdrew from the area and resigned as military chief, to write a famous letter. In fact, the main Cuban leaders had acted without previous agreement, thus making it easier for the anti-Cuban plot fraught by the government of the United States to succeed. Tomás Estrada Palma, the Delegate of the Cuban Revolutionary Party, who reached certain agreements with Washington without first communicating or consulting this with the revolution's civilian and military leadership, was especially to blame.

The United States Take Possession of Cuba

At the beginning of the North-American occupation, General Leonard Wood (1860-1927) was appointed Governor of Oriente. Wood immediately stood out as an aggressive annexationist, and as a man willing to repress the Cuban people. After Santiago de Cuba surrendered, peace negotiations were streamlined. On December 10, 1898, the Treaty of Paris was signed, putting an end to the war. On the one hand, the United States behaved as if Cuba were a conquered territory: it did not recognize Cuban authorities, and treated the people at large as enemies. On the other hand, Spanish colonialist rulers, goaded by revanchism and by the need to defend their own economic interests, chose to discuss matters directly with the North-American negotiators. Thus, the representatives of the Cuban people were not consulted about, much less participated in, the negotiations that led to the signing of the Treaty of Paris. Cuba was entirely handed over to the United States, fully at its disposal, completely restrained. According to the Treaty, Puerto Rico, occupied by North-American troops without firing a shot, became a colony of the United States, that also occupied and established its rule over the archipelago of the Philippines, located in South East Asia on the Pacific Ocean.

Abiding by the Treaty, Spanish colonial authorities handed over power to General John Brooke, appointed as the military governor of Cuba, on January 1, 1899. The old liberators who had fought for thirty years to attain independence, witnessed the hoisting of the North-American flag, instead of the Cuban one, on military fortresses and public buildings. Interventionist forces and numerous Cubans in the service of the new master, launched an intense propaganda campaign about the "generous aid" granted by the United States to Cuba's independence, but neither the people nor the liberators trust imperialist intentions from the start. This lack of trust became more obvious when General Brooke was replaced by General Wood. As the years 1899 and 1900 elapsed, the patriotic spirit intensified and presented a stronger resistance to North-American annexationist projects. Men like Bartolomé Masó, Enrique Collazo, Manuel Sanguily and Salvador Cisneros Betancourt did not conceal their repudiation of North-American policies against Cuba's independence. The government of the United States realized that any attempt to force the annexation of Cuba would be opposed by a resolute and heroic people.

There are numerous testimonies about the willingness to continue the war—that time around against the North-American occupants—and about the almost unanimous rejection of the interventionists and the annexationists. North-American imperialists were obliged to change their policy, abandon their annexationist projects and rule Cuba without including it in the Union, pretending to have fulfilled the urge for independence of the Cuban people.

PART V

1. 20TH CENTURY

Imperialist Domination
Shaping a New Revolutionary Consciousness

Of course Cuba has very little or no independence left after the
Platt Amendment...I believe it is a very desirable acquisition for
the United States. The island will gradually become North
American and, in due time, we will have one of the richest and
most desired possessions in the world...[1]

LEONARD WOOD

Cuba must fear a credit bank more than five battleships.
First come the banks and then the battleships.
They are the banks' shields.[2]

ENRIQUE JOSÉ VARONA

1. Military governor of Cuba, 1899-1902.
2. "Con el eslabón" in *Cuba Contemporánea*, XXIX (La Habana),
1922.

T he Constituent Assembly was convened in 1901. Its apparent task was to have the delegates elected by the Cuban people draft a Constitution. But the summons to the Assembly said that it would also pass an appendix to the Constitution establishing the "right" of the United States to interfere in the internal affairs of the Republic of Cuba. That appendix was the ominous Platt Amendment. Needless to say most delegates refused to approve the text that took independence away from Cuba. The opposition to that imposition from the patriot and Assembly member Juan Gualberto Gómez, is well known. But the North-American government threatened, through General Wood, to indefinitely keep in place the military government in Cuba, to permanently rule Cuba like a North-American military colony. This threat forced many of the enemies of the appendix to vote for it; thus, the 1901 Constitution of the Republic of Cuba was impaired since its inception by the Platt Amendment. Although Cuba was formally independent, North-American imperialists could appoint and remove governments, enjoy all sorts of privileges to invest their money in Cuba and exploit the country's natural and human resources, like in fact they did. It must be said that the Platt Amendment was considered in its time as a partial defeat for the Cuban patriots. However, it was not only that: its inclusion in the Cuban Constitution hindered national sovereignty and, therefore, aroused an even deeper feeling of rejection among the Cuban people. The same happened in regard to the clear mention about the right of the United States—and of conformist Cubans—, to intervene in the country's internal affairs, which emphasized and gave substance to anti-imperialism in the 20th century.

Availing of other mechanisms, imperialists guaranteed their domination over the country. They fostered disunity and contradictions among the liberators since 1898, and preserved the power of former advocates of Spanish colonialism. The Liberation Army was dissolved. Further on, in 1902, Tomás Estrada Palma was imposed as the Republic's president. Estrada Palma won the elections because the other candidate to the presidency, the patriotic General Bartolomé Masó, was excluded from the ballot by North-American military authorities. In 1903, the so-called Trade Reciprocity Treaty was signed, facilitating the entrance of several North-American goods into the Cuban market. Only a few Cuban products, however, were admitted on an equal footing in the North-American market. This mechanism reaffirmed the nature of the Cuban economy as a single-crop producer, on which the absolute predominance of imperialism over Cuba was based. With the Platt Amendment, Tomás Estrada Palma's puppet government, and the Reciprocity Treaty, imperialists had all they needed to dominate Cuba economically and politically.

The historic national project was thwarted from then on. The historical juncture required that a new national movement be formed, strengthened by the economic growth of some productive sectors and of the mass of proletarians who worked with them (in the sugar industry, the railroads and public services), without excluding the groups or class segments who produced goods for daily national consumption.

They had gone back to a situation similar to the one in the late 18th century, in regard to imitating the North-American economic and political order.

Imperialists immediately began to buy land, sugar mills, tobacco factories, railroads and other sources of wealth in Cuba. By 1895, they had invested some fifty million dollars, which rose to more than two-hundred millions in 1909. They deceitfully left pending the fate of the Isle of Pines—that was gradually being populated by North-American landowners—, until a new Treaty was signed at some future stage. They also tried to colonize other areas in the country, bringing in settlers from the United States. General Wood coincided with General Wilson in saying that it would not be long before Cuba became *a part of the United States*. In the language of imperialism, part of the United States meant a North-American colony.

On the pretext of defending the capitals invested in Cuba and protecting the life of North Americans living in the country, the Platt Amendment stipulated the "right" to interfere in the internal affairs of the island. In the years 1906-1909, 1912, 1917-1920, 1933-1934, the government of the United States sent troops and battleships to Cuba and meddled in Cuban affairs. In none of these cases were imperialists acting in good faith, for they were moved by the will to keep their accomplices in power, to crush the Cuban people's rebelliousness. (The unsuccessful economic and political blockade set up after 1959, and the terrorist and military aggressions in more recent years are further proof of the violence that characterizes imperialism).

The False Cuban Governments

Domination by force became evident for the first time during neo-colonial times in 1906. Estrada Palma's government, set up in power by the United States, intended to keep it through abuse and fraud. When the liberals took up arms against this criminal policy, the United States intervened and occupied the island once again. It is true that Estrada Palma's government requested the intervention; but it is also true that, by doing so, it was fulfilling the wishes of the North-American government, that profited from any circumstance to show the inability of the Cuban people to rule democratically. What the North Americans failed to say was that the 1906 uprising was the consequence of the policies implemented by the conservative government they had imposed. From this new intervention emerged Charles Magoon's government, characterized by the use of all possible means to corrupt Cubans and protect national accomplices and North-American adventurers living in Cuba. When Magoon handed over power to president-elect José Miguel Gómez in 1909, incredible sums of money had been squandered in low-quality public works, and the Cuban state was swamped by debts. It is obvious that the "democratizing" and "civilizing" intentions of imperialist interests at the time was as great a lie as it is nowadays.

José Miguel Gómez (1858-1921), known as *Tiburón* (Shark) by his followers, was elected president by the Liberal Party and, although the post of Secretary of State went to Manuel Sanguily (1848-1925), who took a patriotic, firm and honest stand on the face of annexionist and interventionist attempts, Tiburón's government was also characterized by political and administrative corruption. The uprising of the movement called Independientes de Color (Colored Independents, 1912) took place during José Miguel Gómez's term in office. This movement had rallied many black and mulatto Cubans who, under the influence of certain politicians, and without a clear idea of how that battle should be waged, took up arms against racial discrimination. Its main leaders were assassinated. Tiburón's government availed of this development to present himself before the United States and reactionary Cubans as a political team "capable of keeping law and order". Nevertheless, the marines landed in Cuba again.

Tiburón's government was followed by the one headed by Mario García Menocal (1866-1941), whom his political followers and accomplices called El Mayoral (the foreman), to emphasize his conservative, hardline stance. World War I (1914-1918) had already begun, brought about by contradictions between German imperialists, on the one hand, and British, French and North-American imperialists on the other. Washington staunchly supported the aristocratic Menocal, who got himself re-elected as president through electoral fraud in 1917. The liberals took up arms again, like they had in 1906. But this time it was a farce with which both the government and the opposition sought imperialist support for their own lust for power. The government of the United States, on the pretext of the world war and the liberal uprising, sent its marines to Cuba again, where they remained until 1920. They also sent General Enoch Crowder to intervene in political squabbles in the country. Later, this man was appointed ambassador of the United States to Cuba.

During Menocal's two terms in office, the working class began to organize and waged its first great battles. The influence of the October Revolution in Russia, and the extreme poverty in which the Cuban people lived in the midst of the great speculation brought about by the world war, accelerated the rise of the popular movement.

Economic speculation that grew during the war had its effects on Cuba. Several million dollars were invested in the country to gain control of its sugar industry. Foreign and national capitalists spoke about prosperity, but due to foreign economic domination and to the exploitation of the working class, the standards of living of the population at large did not improve, for the prices of foodstuffs, textiles and housing were extremely high. When the war in Europe ended, the United States speculated even further with Cuban sugar, whose value had risen to 20 cents a pound. However, in 1920-1921 the price of sugar suddenly dropped in the New York market, causing a severe crisis in Cuba. Thousands of workers were laid off their jobs; middle-class people lost their businesses and also their savings, for several banks went bankrupt. Logically, this disaster contrasted with the millions amassed by big North-American companies through the sale of Cuban products and the exploitation of Cuban workers. The lean years began, characterized by extreme poverty. It was obvious that the policy of Menocal's government, supported by imperialism, favored the interests of big foreign companies and Cuban businessmen, for it made the working people bear the brunt of the crisis.

The fraudulent "democratic" process under way in Cuba continued. Alfredo Zayas (1861-1934), known as *El Chino* (the Chinaman), was elected president in the elections held in 1921. A shrewd and unscrupulous politician, Zayas was even more corrupt than his predecessors, although he demagogically appeared to tolerate freedom of speech. His performance was tampered with by General Crowder who, on the pretext of fighting against corruption, appointed and removed cabinet members. During Zayas' government, discontent among the working class and the petit-bourgeoisie grew. The working class had waged several battles to improve its living conditions since 1899 when the United States occupied the island, even before Zayas came to power. Certain sections of the liberal petit-bourgeoisie were discontent about increasing political corruption and the extant remains of colonialism. Numerous testimonies from that time disclose the mounting criticisms against North-American domination. Enrique José Varona (1849-1933) outstood among those who spoke against the situation. After the economic crisis in the 1920s, when poverty and political corruption became widespread phenomena, the workers organized in powerful associations like the Railway Brotherhood of Cuba. Numerous students from the recently founded University Students' Federation (FEU, after its name in Spanish), inspired by a great leader: the young Marxist Julio Antonio Mella (1903-1929), began the struggle to transform the country. In fact, revolutionary conditions heightened and became more effective as a consequence of the repercussions of the October socialist revolution, whose example defined the true terms of class struggle at a national level, and of anti-imperialism, prompting the formation of revolutionary Marxist organizations. A younger generation of patriots was in the making. In 1923, revolutionary forces appeared that would address the need of openly struggling against imperialism and of undertaking the task of attaining far-reaching economic and social changes. Zayas' government, availing of demagogy and repression, tried to stop this revolutionary wave. He held elections, characterized by fraud and political abuse, like all previous elections. General Gerardo Machado (1871-1939) won those elections; his demagogical program for "regeneration" camouflaged his deeply embedded reactionary thinking.

Like it always happens, corrupt governments spark discontent; then, another bourgeois politician promises to rectify, but it is only a matter of giving a new face to corruption, and this often entails more repression, on the pretext of reforms carried out by the new government. Haven't Richard Nixon's excesses been criticized by North-American millionaires and their lawyers, who installed him in power and later promoted changes through reforms to apeace domestic unrest and restore the prestige of North-American "democracy," deteriorated by the monopolies' continual frauds and abuses?

Machado's Brutal Dictatorship

The revolutionary wave continued to gain strength. The Communist Party of Cuba and the National Workers' Federation were formed in 1925. North-American imperialism and its domestic accomplices were alarmed by the sugar industry and railway workers' strikes. Machado had stated that he would not allow any strike to last more than 24 hours and, in order to keep his promise, he used every repressive and criminal means available to him. The great communist poet and leader

Rubén Martínez Villena (1899-1934), rightly dubbed Machado a "dunce with claws". As he massacred workers and peasants, Machado also ordered the assassination of some of his political opponents. One year after he was sworn in as president, Machado had proved to be a savage dictator. He intended to remain in that post for more than the four-year period established by the constitution, which he amended in 1928 extending his mandate to six years. He promoted his reelection later on. The student movement was the first one to strongly protest against this extension. The economic crisis worsened; sugar production was restricted and, when salaries were lowered and unemployment rose, the political crisis also became worse. In 1929, Machado ordered the assassination of the courageous revolutionary Julio Antonio Mella who, together with Carlos Baliño, had founded the Communist Party in 1925. Mella was killed in Mexico, where he was living in exile.

It must be borne in mind that, from 1929 until 1934, capitalism worldwide experienced a profound economic and social crisis; even in the United States discontent was the reason why a reformist president—Franklin Delano Roosevelt (1882-1945)—was elected. In 1930, Cuban students, led by the University Students' Directorate (DEU, after its name in Spanish), continued their struggle against Machado's dictatorship. In its turn, the workers' movement carried out huge, combative strikes all along that same year. The influence exerted by the opposition—made up of the traditional bourgeois parties that basically sought to reach an agreement with Machado—was waning. During the struggle, clear-cut Marxist-oriented movements emerged, like the Students' Left Wing and the International Workers Defense, as opposed to democratic, non-Marxist groups like the University Students' Directorate and, more precisely, to the fascist-style organization ABC. The struggle against Machado's dictatorship became a powerful, increasingly larger and deeper national movement.

Machado saw no better alternative to counter the situation than to increase repression and assassinations. Imperialists began to doubt his ability to stop the revolutionary wave and guarantee the safety of their investments in the country. A new North-American ambassador, Sumner Welles, arrived in Havana in 1933. By that time, the armed struggle had broken out in the Cuban countryside. Imperialists offered to act as "mediators" among the various bourgeois political parties in the government and the opposition. Needless to say that neither the Communist Party of Cuba, nor the Workers' Federation, the Directorate, or the newly formed Radical ABC, lent themselves to imperialism's foul play. Ambassador Welles intended to either make Machado hand over power to one of the traditional politicians, or to prompt all bourgeois politicians to reach an agreement that would halt the revolutionary movement. Interventionist negotiations had barely begun, when a strike by transportation workers in Havana spread to small businesses, medical services and other sectors, virtually paralyzing the country. Although this strike was, to a great extent, a spontaneous move, the Communist Party and Rubén Martínez Villena were extraordinarily important actors in its context.

On August 12, 1933, when the entire country was prepared for a decisive confrontation, the army, that had systematically supported Machado, demanded that he resign. Machado fled to the United States, and his cabinet was replaced by a provisional government headed by Carlos Manuel de Céspedes de Quesada, the son of the nation's founding father and a conservative, who had been a diplomat to that date. The provisional government did not take any of the measures that the country's revolutionary situation required and, although this gave rise to more popular discontent, the imperialist plot appeared to have been successful.

On September 4, 1933, the revolutionary movement entered into a new phase. On that day, groups of students and soldiers overthrew Carlos Manuel de Céspedes' government and set up what came to be known as the pentarchy, or the five-men government. Instead of a president, there were five executives, each in charge of a specific branch of state activity. The officers in Machado's army were dismissed. Sergeant Fulgencio Batista was promoted to colonel, and began to rebuild the army with make-shift officers. Neither Batista nor the new officers purported to take any revolutionary measures; all they wanted was to replace the officers dismissed, and enjoy the privileges and perks they had enjoyed in their turn. The pentarchy was dissolved on September 10, and one of the five executives: Ramón Grau San Martín, was appointed as the country's new president. Imperialism tried to put pressure on the revolutionaries by sending their battleships to the island, and threateningly anchoring them near Cuban coasts.

Antonio Guiteras Holmes (1906-1935) was one of the members of Grau San Martín's government. Guiteras was a consistent anti-imperialist fighter who did not belong to any party and had encouraged the armed struggle against Machado. Grau's government was not homogeneous, for its bourgeois and opportunistic elements hampered its ability to function. Furthermore, the power of the army headed by the ambitious Batista grew slowly. Therefore, as the government—prompted by Guiteras—took measures urgently demanded by the people, the army pounced with all its might on the popular movement, like it happened in the case of the "Soviet" formed at the Senado sugar mill, and elsewhere in the country. On September 1933, the revolutionary wave had reached its peak. Several sugar mills in Oriente and Las Villas were seized by the workers who, in some cases, distributed the land among the peasants in the area. The former

Machado's army officers dismissed by the September 4 coup—egged on by the North-American ambassador, and supported by the reactionary ABC organization—, took up arms against Grau's government. In November, there were bloody clashes in Havana and other cities. Despite the fact that the government was able to counter this backward attempt, it was unable to control Batista's growing power. He formed an alliance with the North-American ambassador for a coup d'etat to set up a government entirely submissive to foreign domination. In January 1934, Grau resigned and was replaced by Carlos Mendieta.

The Dictatorship

An increasingly reactionary stage then began. Maneuvers by bourgeois politicians and the repression unleashed by the army and the police corps under Batista's command gradually blocked the popular revolutionary movement that, on the other hand, lacked unity and a clear consciousness of its aims. However, important strikes still took place during 1934-1935.

Bourgeois politicians endeavored to reach an agreement with Batista to hold elections and grant a legal appearance to the situation brought about by the North-American intervention. However, the people were beginning to uphold the calling to convene a Constitutional Assembly that would address the most pressing popular demands, particularly the approval of social legislation confirming what the workers had conquered after more than ten years of struggle and sacrifice. But bourgeois politicians were not interested in convening the Assembly, for popular discontent was such, that they ran the risk of losing control over it. They sought alliances and settlements without consulting the masses, for they would rather hold elections that allowed them to share power. Such elections were held in 1936, and Miguel Mariano Gómez was proclaimed president, supported by dictator Batista. However, disagreements surfaced shortly after, and Miguel Mariano was deposed on that same year.

The 1940 Constitution

The popular movement gained new momentum in 1937. The heroic war waged by the Spanish people against fascism, the progressive measures taken by Lázaro Cárdenas' government in Mexico, and the growing threat of German fascism, contributed to strengthen democratic stances. Batista, pressed on the one hand by the international situation, adverse to North-American imperialism, and on the other hand, threatened by crisis and discontent in Cuba, maneuvered to give its dictatorship a reformist appearance. It was decided to convene the Constituent Assembly in 1940. The participation of the Communist Party and other progressive elements resulted in the recognition of people's rights and the banning of large estates by the Constitution. The observance of those rights, and the implementation of an agrarian reform depended on the approval of specific laws at a future stage. Aware of the fact that the Constitution could not overlook popular conquests, bourgeois politicians, who were the majority in Congress, indefinitely postponed the approval of such laws. Thus, people's rights were included in the Constitution as a merely theoretical statement.

The aim of the bourgeois politicians' maneuvers was to create the illusion of reformism to rally the popular support that would allow them to restrain the revolutionary movement. To counter these maneuvers, Communist Party members succeeded in including provisos in the 1940 Constitution and in other legislation approved later, aimed at improving the standards of living of the poor. But this Constitution—a progressive one in its time—did not provide a real solution to the country's most pressing problems: the concentration of vast expanses of land in the hands of a few, unemployment, illiteracy, foreign domination and other evils that were only eradicated with the triumph of the Revolution in 1959, when the social system that prevailed in the country to that date was radically transformed. Both the 1936 elections and the 1940 Constituent Assembly made a mockery of popular needs. The ruling classes always find a way to make the most of ballot results. Even if the most dispossessed among the people vote for reformists, they do it to achieve reforms and not to let everything go on as it was.

World War II

World War II (1939-1945) began in Europe as a consequence of imperialist rivalries, and soon spread throughout the world. Great Britain and France participated in it, with fascist Germany and Italy as their opponents. The United States became involved in the war later on, siding with the two former powers, as well as Japan, on the fascists' side. Several thousand men were killed in the war, and hundreds of cities were virtually destroyed. German fascists invaded the Soviet Union in 1941. They hated that country—as did all imperialists—and did not want other nations to follow the example set by Soviet workers. It is unnecessary to explain at length the major role of the Soviet people in the destruction of the fascist military machine, at the cost of several million lives and enormous material losses. Cuban governments backed North-American imperialists, while the people, more politically conscious, supported the Soviet Union. Socialism's stance became stronger after the war; liberation movements emerged in Africa and Asia, to that date under colonialist domination.

We have witnessed in our time the courageous and victorious struggle of those peoples, which no one could restrain or stop. The Cuban Revolution is placed in the context of that revolutionary wave. The Cuban people's struggle has always been set in the great junctures of colonial aggression and liberation. There were patriotic conspiracies between 1810 and 1830, coinciding with the struggle in Latin-American countries that wanted to rid themselves of Spanish colonialism. From 1868 until 1880, when Cuba was waging its wars of independence, a colonialist offensive was launched in Asia and Africa, sparking the peoples' resistance. In 1871, the French people set up the Paris Commune. And in 1895, as Cuba pursued its war of independence, imperialism began to make itself felt. The great José Martí issued warnings about and struggled against its expansionist intentions. After 1945, capitalism faced a new political and social crisis in whose context the more developed, more united and more conscious Cuban people attained its definitive independence on January 1, 1959.

Reaction, Corruption and a New Dictatorship

The governments of Batista (1940-1944), Ramón Grau San Martín (1944-1948) and Carlos Prío (1948-1952) were characterized by widespread corruption; they speculated at the expense of the people throughout World War II. All of them were demagogical and suppressed popular movements. Between 1940 and 1944, the crisis in Cuba due to the struggle against fascism, that had spread the imperialist war worldwide, increasingly burdened the Cuban people. The situation caused by limited economic development and continual foreign exploitation, gradually became evident.

The demagogical "authentics"—a name given to politicians from the (Authentic) Cuban Revolutionary Party during Grau and Prío's governments—, were unable to restrain the nascent revolutionary wave; on the contrary, it was clear to the Cuban people that neither dictatorship nor bourgeois democracy with its fraudulent elections could solve the country's problems, but rather worsened them. During "authentic" governments, the students, young middle-class people and members of the workers' movement, were constantly harassed. Following imperialism's orders, workers' leaders Jesús Menéndez and Aracelio Iglesias were assassinated in 1948.

After the war, and specially since 1948, the international situation clearly indicated that North-American imperialism was getting ready to set up puppet dictatorships in Latin America that would support its onslaught against the peoples and socialism. Part of the Cuban bourgeoisie and its politicians, among them President Prío himself, feared that the Orthodox Party would win the next elections, thus allowing the people to thwart their plans. The situation seemed so explosive that not even the suicide of orthodox leader Eduardo Chibás assuaged their fears. Late in 1951, there ensued a new period of economic depression in Cuba, due to a price fall in the sugar market. Batista began to conspire with a group of army officers and on March 10, 1952, supported by the United States, he led a coup d'etat. President Prío and most of his closest associates did not put up any resistance whatsoever, and fled from the country, relinquishing power to the conspirators.

Cultural Maturity

Since José Martí had turned 19th century Cuban cultural heritage into a mighty political weapon, the phony Republic proclaimed in 1902 witnessed a scientific and literary renaissance, based on criticism of social and political practices, on research about what was peculiarly Cuban, and on protests against foreign domination. This was what characterized the works by Enrique José Varona and Manuel Sanguily, who fought in the 19th century wars of liberation. Other younger authors— like Fernando Ortiz (1881-1969), an ethnohistorian who did research on black culture in Cuba; Ramiro Guerra (1881-1970), who reformed historical research; the novelists Miguel de Carrión (1875-1929) and Carlos Loveira (1882-1928), and the poets José Manuel Poveda (1888-1926) and Regino Boti (1878-1958)—, inspired by positivism, naturalism and modernism, gave new momentum to national culture. In 1913, in his book *Contra el yanqui* (Against the Yankee), Julio César Gandarilla proposed nationalizing foreign properties. The magazine *Cuba Contemporánea* (Contemporary Cuba, 1914-1917) and the *Revista Bimestre Cubana* (Cuban Bi-monthly Review, 1910-1969), were already being published before 1930.

As these intellectuals retook and developed national themes, a new generation was in the making that, besides reaching a higher expressive quality, contributed with the revolutionary, progressive and Marxist messages of its most outstanding exponents. Rubén Martínez Villena, a unique poet; Juan Marinello (1898-1977), who left an extensive and valuable work inspired on Martí; María Villar Buceta, of a unique poetic expression; Regino Pedroso (born in 1896), the first one to directly depict the proletariat in Cuban poetry; Nicolás Guillén (1902-1990), the first one to include black elements in Cuban literature, decisively contributing to its strength and character; Alejo Carpentier (1904-1980), a master of narrative, who significantly approached the so-called black themes, and many others, were a clearly defined group of creators whose works are essential to understand more recent historical developments in Cuba. There were also great innovators in visual arts, like Víctor Manuel and Eduardo Abela (1892-1965) who, together with the great musicians Amadeo Roldán (1900-1939) and Alejandro García Caturla (1906-1940), destroyed the academic, imitative artistic tradition. In his turn, historian Emilio Roig de Leuchsenring (1889-1964) showed the hypocrisy of imperialist "aid" and popularized the knowledge of the history of the liberation struggle through the Cuban Society of Historic and International Studies, founded in 1940. The *Revista de Avance* (Advance Review, 1927-1930) and the Grupo Minorista (Minority Group) were the harbingers of the creative work by that generation, whose results and influence are very much alive to this date.

PART VI

2. 20TH CENTURY

The Armed Struggle (1953-1958)
The Revolution
On the Road to Socialism (1959-1986)

When we speak about struggle, we mean by people the great
rebellious masses to whom everyone makes promises and whom
everyone cheats and betrays; the people who want a better,
more honorable and more just fatherland; the people moved by
age-old aspirations of justice, for they have suffered from
injustice and mockery one generation after another; the people
who want far-reaching and intelligent changes and, to achieve
them—when they believe in something or in someone, but
mainly when they believe in themselves—are willing to give
their last drop of blood.[1]

The objectives in the agenda were fulfilled and proclaimed at
every stage, for the revolutionary movement and the people had
attained the required maturity.[2]

FIDEL CASTRO

1. *History Will Absolve Me* (1953).
2. *Report to the First Congress of the Communist Party of Cuba,* 1975.

A new stage began, characterized by the rapid growth of a powerful revolutionary movement, and the worsening of all negative economic and political traits. Batista became a servile supporter of imperialism's international activity, which included a brutal onslaught against Latin America, symbolized by the aggression to Jacobo Arbenz's government in Guatemala, and against socialism by means of the so-called "cold war". In Cuba, Batista violently repressed the workers' movement and the revolutionaries. His adventurous and mindless economic policy, that only benefitted foreign capitalists and a few Cubans, as well as the corrupt members of his cabinet, far for solving the country's grave problems, made them even worse. Meanwhile, Batista crushed all popular protests availing, on the one hand, of the police corps and, on the other, of a group of corrupt trade union leaders in his payroll. But the masses could not continue to bear the brunt of the crisis of neocolonialism, and an armed vanguard emerged from within the people.

The struggle began on July 26, 1953, when Fidel Castro and a group of young men attacked the Moncada Garrison in Santiago de Cuba. Their aim was to arm the people and overthrow the dictatorship after seizing the garrison. On that same day, another group of young men attacked the garrison in Bayamo. The tyrant's army controlled the situation by massacring the young revolutionaries. During the trial held by the tyranny against Fidel and his companions-in-arms, he undertook his self-defense, expounding the people's right to make the revolution against the dictatorship, denouncing the extreme poverty in which the people lived, and the corruption of the ruling classes. The document he presented to the court arguing his case, entitled *History Will Absolve Me*, mirrors the terrible conditions in which Cuba lived in those days, as well as the profound social ideas that moved the revolutionaries. This document makes it is easy to understand why, based on that program, the revolution opted for socialism, carrying out the unavoidable transformations it envisaged. The attack on the Moncada Garrison was the spark that strengthened and guided the revolutionary movement. Conditions were mature for a decisive struggle.

In 1955, the struggle of the workers' movement had developed tremendously, and the national movement for the release of political prisoners forced the dictator to set them free, including the participants in the attack against the Moncada Garrison, imprisoned in the Isle of Pines. Fidel and his companions had to leave the country due to the dictatorship's repeated threats. They settled in Mexico and began to organize and train a group of men. They bought a small yacht, the *Granma*, that brought eighty-two expeditionaries to the Coloradas, in what is currently Granma province, on December 2, 1956. The November 30 uprising in Santiago de Cuba, led by Frank País, showed there existed an important and strong rearguard that supported the preparations for the armed struggle.

After the first clashes with the dictator's army, only twelve expeditionaries were able to continue fighting. They succeeded in going deep into the Sierra Maestra where, aided by the peasants, they began to organize the combative Rebel Army. In 1957, the Cuban people learned about the armed struggle being waged in the mountains, and that Batista's army had been defeated in several combats. The dictator tried to buy time, promising to hold elections, as hundreds of combatants emerged from the people to wage daily battles in the cities; all consistent revolutionaries who acknowledged the Rebel Army as their main advanced guard, gradually united. Armed protest movements and strikes in the cities—like the ones that took place in August and September 1957, and in

April 1958, mainly in Cienfuegos and Sagua La Grande—showed that repression was unable to restrain the revolutionary wave. The armed struggle came to its final stage after the failure of the offensive launched by the dictatorship's forces in the Sierra Maestra against the Rebel Army; the creation of the Second Front Frank País, under Commander Raúl Castro, in the northern area of the former Oriente province, and the spreading of guerrilla warfare to other areas. The columns under the command of Camilo Cienfuegos (1932-1959) and Ernesto Che Guevara (1928-1967) crossed the former Camagüey province and entered Las Villas after a heroic march, dealing a decisive blow against the dictatorship in the country's central region, by taking the town of Yaguajay and the city of Santa Clara. In Oriente, the Rebel Army, under Commander-in-Chief Fidel Castro, launched an offensive in November 1958 and, in December, it occupied strategically important towns like Palma Soriano, La Maya, and others.

In December, after seizing several towns and cities, the Rebel Army laid siege on Santiago de Cuba and Santa Clara in the provinces of Oriente and Las Villas, respectively. The dictatorship's army was demoralized, its officers were corrupt and inept, and the aid coming from the United States could not help defeat the revolutionary army; dictator Batista and his accomplices fled from the country in a panic on January 1, 1959.

If the two years of armed struggle in the Sierra Maestra and in the cities are worth mentioning as military, organizational and heroic feats, it is equally true that the Rebel Army implemented in the territories it controlled, setting an example with its own behavior, a series of measures that the revolution would implement at a national level as soon as it took over power. The anti-illiteracy campaign, the political education of peasants and combatants, the approval of a decree to implement the agrarian reform, as well as the respect for the population at large, including the defeated troops, heralded the profound changes that took place since January 1, 1959. What happened on that day? The same thing that had happened before: several pseudo-leaders attempted to appropriate the people's victory. A maneuver backed by army officers and a group of bourgeois politicians purported to establish a government in Havana, where the entire population responded to the order for a general strike issued by the Rebel Army's headquarters in Oriente. A revolutionary government was set up in Santiago de Cuba, the first step toward taking over power in the country. But this time around, the people were not deceived.

The Revolution

A new stage began in Cuba's history. A complete transformation began to take place in the life of the Cuban people. This revolution was the clarion call that announced a further stage of liberation to the world. For the first time in the history of the Americas, a people, in continual communication with its leaders, participated without hindrances in the policy-making process and in specific measures to implement it. Since January 1, 1959, Cuba swiftly changed. The entire people, supporting its leaders, took the path of creative work, of the struggle against poverty, ignorance, corruption, vice and national and foreign exploiters, for education, welfare, health and international solidarity. Production was prioritized. Centuries of exploitation had to be obliterated. The revolution paved the way to new possibilities for national development and for a more just and happier society. The first thing the revolutionary forces did was to destroy the military and police apparatus that had been used by Batista's dictatorship, as well as by foreign and national exploiters to abuse the Cuban people, steal the product of their work and persecute and assassinate them when they protested.

The army and the forces of repression that existed in January 1, 1959, when the revolution triumphed, were quickly dissolved. The most strategically important points throughout the island were occupied by the Rebel Army that, since the first days of that year, became the most faithful guardian of the revolution. But still more needed to be done, like punishing the dictatorship's accomplices who had murdered peasants, workers, students, men, women and children. The revolution took them to trial, where proof of their crimes was presented, and they were punished according to the graveness of their offenses. It was essential to do this because the experience of the Cuban people—and also of peoples elsewhere—shows that the tools used by the exploiters must be completely destroyed if the people really want its revolution to triumph, to introduce radical changes in history.

Numerous popular needs also had to be met. That is why measures were taken to benefit the workers and the poor. New jobs had to be created; the unemployed had to be given work. Cuban workers believed that the country could no longer live almost exclusively from producing and selling sugar. It was necessary to improve the workers and employees' standards of living as well. Salaries were raised. Capitalists not only exploited the people, paying very low salaries, but also charging quite high prices for rent, medicine and other essential goods and various services. The revolution lowered rents and the price of medicines, and some services like electricity, in the hands of an imperialist company that reaped enormous profits. All these measures met urgent needs, but were not enough to transform the country. It was necessary, therefore, to take measures aimed at eliminating the exploiters' economic power and at eradicating unemployment, illiteracy and the lack of medical services in the countryside. Thousands of peasants were jobless, others only worked two of three months each year, during the sugar cane harvest; there were more than a hundred thousand landless peasants. An agrarian reform was required in order to improve the peasants' living conditions.

On the Road to Socialism (1959-1986)

On May 17, 1959, the tenets stating that the land should belong to those who tilled it, that no one should own uncultured land, that no one had the right to charge rent to peasants for the land they cultivated, were validated by a bill approved on that date. According to the newly passed law, farms in Cuba could not exceed thirty *caballerías* (1 caballería = 33 acres). It was decided that no peasant would pay rent for the land he and his family tilled. Big landowners, who possessed large expanses of land, protested against this law. They knew that if land was distributed among the peasants, they would lose all their economic and political clout. Big foreign companies, egged on by the United States ambassador to Cuba, also opposed this just law and, wielding all sorts of threats, opposed the agrarian reform. The Revolution readied to face its enemies. The people organized the revolutionary militia that paraded in Havana for the first time on May 1, 1959. The revolutionary people of Cuba countered the obstacles put in place by foreign and national interests with the slogan "The Agrarian Reform is on!," voiced by thousands countrywide.

The people knew this was the first step toward real changes in the country. And the revolutionary leadership understood not only the need to implement the agrarian reform by defeating every enemy, but also that the struggle against those enemies would become more necessary and more violent with each passing day. The National Agrarian Reform Institute (INRA, after its name in Spanish), chaired by Fidel, organized agrarian development zones, headed by seasoned combatants of the Rebel Army. As a result of the implementation of the agrarian reform, more than one hundred thousand landless peasants who, to that date had been unable to freely enjoy the fruits of their work, were given the deeds to their land. The big foreign companies lost theirs, which was placed under state management, on behalf of the entire nation, but specially of agricultural workers who had been exploited for such a long time in those same estates. People's farms were established at that time.

The agrarian reform weakened the most powerful exploiters' groups in Cuba. By mid-1959, these groups attacked the revolution availing of the reactionary national and foreign media, organized sabotages, machine-gunned cities and facilities and, above all, hampered production. The interests that had prevailed to that date shared the imperialists' and the big landowners' aggressive attitude. Groups of counterrevolutionaries funded by imperialism made public threats about military intervention, but they only succeeded in strengthening the revolution and accelerating the process under way, for those actions contributed to the people's political education. The year 1960 was intensively dramatic for the Cuban Revolution, that upheld its stance even more firmly than ever before, fully aware of itself and of its possibilities. In this regard, the revolution's leadership—and the entire Cuban people—had realized that, in order to safeguard the measures already taken by the Revolution, aimed at administering social justice and welfare and achieving economic development, as well as others it would adopt in the future, it was imperative to take economic power away from the exploiters, to deprive them of the land, the industries, the railways, the warehouses, the banks they used to fleece the people, plunder the country's natural resources and rule in connivance with successive governments and other allies.

Consequently, the revolution had to take more stringent measures. Each imperialist aggression received a more radical response. Thus, when the government of the United States stopped buying Cuban sugar, the revolutionary government nationalized various capitalist enterprises. The people adopted the slogan "No Quota, But No Master". When oil companies threatened to ground the country to a halt for lack of fuel, the revolutionary government nationalized those companies. In those two occasions, Cuba received the solidary support of the Soviet Union, that bought the sugar and supplied the oil the Cuban industry needed. After these measures were taken, imperialist aggressions increased. National and foreign ruling classes had not been deprived of most of their economic power. On the island, they had allies who served their political aims and increased the acts of sabotage against production. The attempt against the ship *La Coubre*, that brought a cargo of arms to defend the revolution, unmasked imperialism's criminal intentions. It was imperative to nip the enemy's might in the bud and, between July and October 1960, big industries, trade and banks were nationalized. By taking over production and finances countrywide, the revolutionary government was not only capable of defending itself from aggressions, but also of putting into practice an economic plan to streamline development according to the people's needs. The Urban Reform Law put an end to the exploitation by urban real estate owners.

Consequently, imperialism and its national allies increased their attacks. By late 1960, the people of Cuba approved the First Declaration of Havana (September 2, 1960). The declaration denounced the agreements taken by the Organization of American States, pointed at North-American imperialists as the enemies of peace and of the American peoples and stated that the governments that supported the aggression against Cuba were betraying their own peoples.

In January 1961, the government of the United States decided to withdraw its diplomatic and consular representatives from Cuba, thinking this would instil fear into the people and their leadership. The policy of direct armed aggression and of economic blockade was thus inaugurated, for the breaking of diplomatic and consular relations meant that practically all trade between the two countries ceased. At that time, Cuba strengthened its links with the socialist countries. Once the problem was posed in these terms, the Revolution, that had intensified its defense mechanisms, supported by the armed people, began to organize the country in a more adequate fashion, for the administrative and leadership structures inherited from capitalism were unfit to face and resolve the problems of economic planning. As the agrarian reform was implemented in agrarian development zones, the industry was organized in large units, and the groundwork was laid for the creation of the Ministry of Industries. On the other hand, Cuban workers, aware that it was essential to invest resources in development, took the initiative of restricting the policy aimed at raising salaries, voluntarily contributed 4 % of their wages to a recently created fund for industrialization, and actively participated in the tasks to organize and manage the economy. Workers also began to work in the countryside, mobilizing voluntarily during sugar cane harvests.

Bearing in mind that the country's economic and social development required that all workers be trained, 1961 was devoted to eliminate illiteracy among the people, a task that mobilized thousands of Cubans, young and old, men and women, who succeeded in lowering illiteracy rates among the total population to 4% in only nine months. Illiteracy had spread unchecked in Cuba to that date. According to estimates, it had reached 30 %, and in some rural areas, it was more than 60%.

Imperialism deemed the moment had arrived to launch the aggression it had been planning for two years and, in April 1961, it tried to destroy the revolutionary power by means of air raids followed by the landing of a mercenary army in Playa Girón. The story is well known. The mercenaries were swiftly defeated: in just three days they were forced to surrender (April 17-19, 1961). Imperialism had suffered an exemplary defeat, and Cuba showed its brothers in the Americas that a revolutionary people, led by revolutionaries, can vanquish its enemies anywhere. On April 16, 1961, Prime Minister and Commander-in-Chief Fidel Castro voiced the Cuban people's will to create, develop and consolidate the first socialist state in Latin America. The Cuban people reasserted its will to blaze its own new trail. Once the enemy had been defeated, it was imperative to direct all efforts to domestic development, without neglecting defense. That is why 1962 marked one of the first major stages in the nation's development. Much energy was devoted on that year to outlining national policies and organizing the state apparatus; as consciousness developed, substantial changes began to be introduced in the agrarian organization born from the implementation of the Agrarian Reform Law. State farms improved. The National Association of Small Farmers (ANAP, initials in Spanish) clearly defined its tasks in regard to peasants. Finally, the economic plan was discussed by all levels involved in production; the working masses participated in those debates. If we bring these facts to mind, and compare them with current productive, organizational, political and cultural achievements, we will realize how much we have gained in experience, and how clearly the Cuban people is now able to see where problems lie and how to solve them.

The imperialists and the counterrevolutionaries then unleashed a new aggression. Armed gangs that had appeared late in 1960, tried to strengthen their positions in the Escambray mountains and elsewhere in the country. Their vandalic actions and the murders they committed were to no avail. The militia and the Rebel Army quickly rid the Escambray and the other areas of those gangs.

Cuba responded to new and repeated aggressions with the Second Declaration of Havana (February 4, 1962), that explained why Latin-American peoples should make their own revolutions, and offered the solidarity of the Cuban people to that endeavor. Later, the United States blocked Cuban territorial waters with its fleet, threatening the Cuban people and the whole world with its atomic weapons. The missile crisis ensued in October 1962; Fidel and the people remained firm, retaliating blow by blow.

The experience gained by the implementation of the agrarian reform, specially in regard to the contrary attitude adopted by landowners that still remained in Cuba, demanded new measures. That is why in 1963, a second and final agrarian reform was implemented. The first agrarian reform had allowed some landowners to keep more than five caballerías; some even owned up to 30 caballerías. Many of the latter did not exploit their land adequately; some did not care if production diminished, and others supported the counterrevolutionaries. It was a section of the population whose attitude was increasingly adverse to the country's development plans. Therefore, the second agrarian reform eliminated farms of more than five *caballerías*, and their owners were paid what the excess land was worth, as compensation.

Once structural changes had concluded, people's mobilizations for the defense and to work in the countryside had increased, and the process of creating new mechanisms and guidelines had advanced, the revolution began to lay down the groundwork for the construction of socialism. It is worth mentioning that, all along that process, and as a sign of popular support, organizations were created and developed, aimed at undertaking the various revolutionary tasks. The National Revolutionary Militia was created in October 26, 1959; the Federation of Cuban Women on August 23, 1960; the Committees for the Defense of the Revolution, on September 28, 1960; the Pioneers' Union, on April 4, 1961; the National Association of Small Farmers, on May 17, 1961, and the Union of Young Communists, on July 15, 1963.

Work in the economic plan was furthered in 1964, leading to the development of areas particularly fit for certain crops. To that date, the emphasis on the country's agricultural development was a basic guideline of the Revolution; economic planning then granted that economic guideline a central role in all national activity. In this context, sugar production had—and still has—pride of place, for it is the largest hard-currency earner in the country.

Experience led to the creation of specialized agricultural plans in areas where no major economic or social development had been previously registered. Therefore, economic structures nationwide were placed on an equal footing. The plans for the Isle of Pines, Girón in Matanzas province, the Sancti Spíritus area, Gran Tierra in northern Oriente province, and many other regions, were streamlined. There is practically no place on the island nowadays that has not been touched by the revolution's creative work.

What was the purpose of developing these areas? The main purpose was to take the revolution and economic progress to them. A few years ago, some of them were virtually uninhabited, isolated, practically paralyzed. Economic progress also meant schools, medical services, sports, recreation and cultural activities for the peasants, so they could fully participate in productive tasks. Some of these plans are based on cash crop plantations, like coffee, citrus fruit and other fruit-bearing trees. There are also special plans devoted to developing other crops, like rice. Animal husbandry has also been developed, based on a special breed of cattle that yields milk, meat and its by-products. The revolution's all-encompassing plans, and specific regional conditions are always borne in mind.

In a few years, these plans have become stronger and are contributing to shape a more coherent economic structure, as well as to effectively diversify production. An essential step was thus taken toward creating a more balanced economy, that allows the Revolution to carry out a global development plan. Another measure required to render the plan fully efficient, was to transform sugar cane agriculture and modernize the sugar industry. A special development plan for this branch was prepared, aimed at making a 10-million tons harvest in 1970. To attain this goal, the country's main sugar mills had to be renovated, their equipment improved, and the sugar harvest, mechanized. On that year, as it is known, the sugar harvest was eight million and a half tons. This reaffirmed the ability of the Cuban people to achieve ambitious goals, and made it possible to attain a higher degree of organization than the one prevailing to that date, that matched the country's level of development. Ever since that time, in which extraordinary efforts were displayed, sugar cane collection centers—where sugar cane is cleaned and cut into pieces before taking it to the mills—, mechanical harvesters and the drive to perfect the harvesters, have become crucial factors in the development of the sugar industry to this date. Thus, efforts displayed since 1966 to raise productivity were furthered with the establishment of a rational cane-cutting system and by mobilizing only the best voluntary cutters. On the year 1970, a higher stage, that of mechanization, was inaugurated.

The basic infrastructure for agriculture and cattle breeding was built countrywide on that year. The dams, large and small, stand out in that context. They form a network of reservoirs of paramount importance for a country like Cuba, subject to prolonged droughts and lacking large rivers.

Industrial development, that includes major thermoelectric plants like those in Mariel, Cienfuegos, Nuevitas and Santiago de Cuba, as well as cement, fertilizer and other factories, deserves a separate mention, as do the harvester-manufacturing plant in Holguín and the pipe factory in Manzanillo, both recently built within the framework of industrial development aimed at meeting the needs of agriculture. Microbrigades have granted momentum to the construction of houses for workers. Another urgent collective need has been met by perfecting and furthering the assembly of buses for urban transportation. Finally, schools—specially secondary and preuniversity and polytechnic schools, as well as teacher-training centers—are also being built, based on the consistent integration of learning and productive work, inspired in the ideas expounded by José Martí and, naturally, by the founders of Marxism-Leninism. These schools purport to form youth by means of active participation in the most pressing, basic tasks for development, contributing to make them understand the collective effort displayed to achieve that goal, and their own role in those efforts and in the practical application of the knowledge they acquire at school. Other variants of the same principle are applied in teacher-training centers, primary schools with vegetable gardens and even in professional higher education. It could be said it is applied in all levels of schooling.

Clearly defined guidelines were established at the 13th Workers' Congress of the Cuban Trade Unions (CTC, after its name in Spanish), well-defined guidelines were set up about organization and participation, aimed at promoting productivity based on the social consciousness promoted by the experience gained and the sacrifices made throughout one decade.

Culture goes hand in hand with these achievements. Individual creation stands out, as does the growing massive cultural activity that nurtures it. The extraordinary production of publications, that exceeds 30 million copies per year; the growth of Cuba's National Ballet; the momentum gained by visual arts, specially posters; the appearance of young musicians and composers of obvious quality; the yearly holding of contests to discover new talents; the unique work carried out at a continental level by Casa de las Américas (the House of the Americas); the popular artists' festivals, attended by thousands of Cubans, indicate the drive towards self-improvement brought about by material and institutional transformations. The arts which, as Juan Marinello ascertained, allow everyone to be the master of their own creativity and their own gifts, together with the swift development of various university specialties, and scientific and technical research, have followed on the footsteps of the anti-illiteracy campaign which paved the way to massive education. The university was reorganized in order to promote specialization; numerous careers were included in the curriculum, specially in the case of exact, natural and social sciences and technology. The creation of institutions like the Academy of Sciences, the National Center for Scientific Research, and the special institutes that deal with the most pressing issues associated to social, political and economic development on the island, was also quite important.

Since its inception, the revolution made huge efforts to promote deep changes in social consciousness and to reassert national sentiments. The confrontation with class enemies, the defense of the revolution, the practice of proletarian internationalism, the development of Marxism-Leninism that indissolubly joins together theory and practice, were the fitting framework for the tasks aimed at development undertaken since 1959. The revolutionary leadership, under the inspiration and guidance of comrade Fidel Castro, always pointed at the path to follow and at the need of proposing more adequate goals for each of the country's stages of development.

After 1970, the revolution's experience and its capacity for self-criticism centered in a project that encompassed, on equal footing, two processes necessarily linked to one another: to organize workers and people's participation in making and putting policy into practice, and to institutionalize state activity. After the 13th Workers' Congress, the people at large were organized in national trade unions, that functioned in every major branch. The process immediately began to prepare the elections to create the organs of People's Power and the Assemblies at all levels. The elections held in Matanzas province in 1974, were an undoubtedly successful test.

The process under way was culminated and defined by the summons to the First Congress of the Communist Party of Cuba. On the one hand, the Party's program of action was drafted, and its thesis were debated by all its members and by the people at large. On the other hand, the first draft of a new Constitution was prepared and discussed nationwide. Hundreds of proposals about the text to be approved emerged from those debates, some of them included in the document's final version. When the Party's First Congress was held in December 1975, it was evident that the people understood the principles and purposes that inspired it. It was precisely the First Congress of the Communist Party that marked the transition to the construction of socialism. The outlines for the development of all national activity were defined at this gathering, whose keynote document was the Report by the First Secretary of the Party, comrade Fidel Castro, who made a lengthy, in-depth analysis of the Revolution's historical background and achievements in each sector, as well as of future perspectives.

Among the agreements adopted by the Party Congress, the ones related to economic planning; the approval of the Republic's Constitution after it had been broadly discussed by the masses; the inauguration of a system of representation through elections held from the municipal level up to the national level (the National Assembly began its working sessions on December 2, 1976); the establishment of a political and administrative territorial division in keeping with local development deserve a special mention, as do the resolutions about all other national activities, that contributed to show the maturity of the revolutionary process, faced with new tasks during the First Five-Year Plan (1976-1980).

It must be borne in mind that, since 1960, socialist countries, led by the Union of Soviet Socialist Republics, and the revolutionary and progressive peoples of the entire world, have supported us decisively, and have contributed, with their encouraging solidarity, to strengthen our determination. This aid from the Soviet Union and the socialist countries also allowed us to develop the Revolutionary Armed Forces to defend the fatherland and the conquests of socialism. The voice of revolutionary Cuba is heeded attentively in all international gatherings. Our words are supported by obviously undeniable facts and achievements, and by its loyalty to the principles of socialism and proletarian internationalism, which Cuba will never renounce.

The Party's Second Congress (1980), emphasized the need to strengthen economy planning in order to organize production and services on an efficient and diversified basis, and to meet the needs of the rapid domestic development and create funds for export, required to replace imports and satisfy foreign markets. It also reiterated the thesis approved in its first gathering (1975), underlining the need to make use of criticism; reaffirmed the revolution's internationalist calling, focused at the time on Angola, Ethiopia and Nicaragua, and its will to maintain its policy for peace and non-alignment; emphasized the need to broaden and improve social services, like education and health, to guide scientific development linked to the requirements of the social and economic level already reached, and to improve production and construction infrastructures.

Between 1985—the year in which the Third Party Congress was held—and December 1986, when the party held an extraordinary working session, some conceptual and practical distortions were perceived in the implementation of economy planning guidelines. Fidel Castro, Chairman of the Council of State and First Secretary of the Party, publicly warned about and analyzed these grave alterations of principles and methods, as mistakes that should be eliminated. The stage known as rectification began. Fidel characterized the nascent negative trends, urging that they be clarified and amended. His speeches showed the path to follow in order to attain a better honed social and individual consciousness. Rectification was carried out energetically and enthusiastically, avoiding unnecessary extremes and within a specifically Cuban framework.

Together with this, an analysis about the huge foreign debt of the so-called Third World, contained in the book *La crisis económica y social del mundo* (Economic and Social Crisis in the World), published by Fidel in 1983, shortly before the 7th Non-Aligned Summit, was widely spread. Three years later, that debt had acquired colossal proportions, specially due to the extortionary policy of North-American imperialist interests. Its origins, and the fact that servicing it cancels every possibility of development, mean that this debt can even provoke social disturbances due to the peoples' increasing poverty. It has been stated at international gatherings held in Cuba and abroad, that such a debt cannot not be serviced and is morally wrong to demand that it be paid. It has been pointed out that Latin America must act jointly to promote its integration, thus emphasizing relationships aimed at overall development and at strengthening common stances at international negotiations.

If we look within the process of rectification, it will be evident that work was continually perfected throughout the country, in the framework of developing national activities even though, as Fidel warned in his speeches, socialist consciousness in regard to work should neither be rushed nor become an element of change as disturbing as the mistakes that justified it. It is rather the will to continue to struggle against what is wrong. And if we look abroad, it will be obvious that the Cuban people did not hold out a friendly hand in vain or reluctantly to the Angolan people and, consequently, to the Namibian people as well.

Science and culture, at the service of a dignified existence at a world level, successfully worked to achieve these goals. The evidence of their quality, and the quality of their message show the transforming force that urges them to achieve further aims. Cuba will continue to oppose its indomitable determination to imperialist aggressions.

The measures adopted in the following years to attain sustained development proved to be insufficient and too complex in regard to guaranteeing the growth of certain sectors, for scientists and technicians of every qualification abounded that could guarantee bigger successes. Before the Third Congress (1985), Fidel presented the more weighty issues, bearing in mind the experience attained during the previous five years, and pointed out that the main task was to perfect methods, procedures and solutions able to eliminate mechanical interpretations and the slow implementation of the plan. Successes attained indicated it was not only possible but inevitable to progress beyond what had been already achieved. It would not be sensible or truthful to believe that a substantial transformation like the one that took place in Cuba would be immutable, remaining deaf and blind to the requirements of each of its various stages.

The extremely difficult international scenario suddenly engulfed certain socialist countries, specially the Soviet Union, consequently determining an essential lack of source of exchange and funding based on national production.

The changes that took place in eastern Europe, involving free market and even privatization of industries and land, as well as the disturbances they caused in regard to economic exchange, specially in the Soviet Union, gradually but intensely reflected on the supplies of fuel and raw materials and on the imports of agricultural products. The Cuban people had to replace, with renewed efforts and ingenuity, the shortages provoked not by their own problems, but generated by other historical conditionings. It had to make the most of available foreign resources and of national materials and products to maintain social consumption, replace the goods it used to import, and increase export funds. After the Congress, work was organized in contingents, the microbrigades were reestablished, the plan aimed at producing foodstuffs was prioritized, as was the production of medicines—some of hem unique in the world, as is the case of the vaccine against eningitis B—, and of certain equipment. The Fourth Congress, held in 1991, addressed these issues and noticed that he plan had been almost entirely accomplished. The Congress also drafted the principles and the priority guidelines or the current special period. To preserve the basic principles of the revolution, rooted in the one-hundred years old radition of independence and sovereignty, overcome current difficulties and vie for a total national development in he future were the Congress central issues. Sensible and cautious steps were taken to attract not directly committed or, in ny case, secondary investments, paving the way to the entrance of hard currency funds into the country. Consequently, ertain major sections of civil society—like more or less conventional religions like Christianity—, began to participate ore actively. Therefore, Cuban civil society has perfected tself inside and out, for this must be one of the main pillars n which to build the future. We will not be deterred from winning our spirit back" like Martí said. Once again, faced y immediately pressing obstacles, Cubans have responded o Fidel's appeal, to the everlasting echo of Che Guevara's ords: Onward to victory, forever!

STATISTICAL SUMMARY

Population
Public Health
Education
Culture and the Arts
Sports

Table 1. Population

Years	Total population	Men	Women
1958	6, 824, 542	3, 506, 718	3, 317, 824
1994	10, 962, 959	5, 505, 622	5, 457, 337

Table 2. Public Health

	1958	1994
Physicians	6, 286	54, 065
Dentists	250	8, 834
Family physicians	0	25, 055
% of people under the care of family physicians	0	94
Infant mortality rate per 1 000 live births	60.0	10.3

Table 3. Education

Educational levels	Registration		Schools	
	1958-59	1994-95	1958-59	1994-95
Primary education	625, 729	1, 007, 769	7, 567*	9, 425
Secondary education	88, 135	674, 152	81	1, 805
Higher education	2, 063**	140, 815	3	33

* Excluding the private sector.

** The figures refer only to private universities; public universities did not work during that year.

Table 4. Culture and the Arts

	1957	1994
Libraries	*	355
Books published	467	3, 691.3
Movies produced	1	21
Museums	6	215
Culture houses	0	266
Art galleries	*	126

* No official data available.

Table 5. Sports

Medals Won by Cuba

	Total	Gold	Silver	Bronze
Central American and Caribbean Games				
X Puerto Rico, 1966	78	33	19	26
XI Panama, 1970	210	98	61	51
XII Dominican Republic, 1974	191	101	55	35
XIII Colombia, 1978	182	120	44	18
XIV Cuba, 1982	282	173	71	38
XV Dominican Republic, 1986	299	174	81	44
XVI Mexico, 1990	322	180	90	52
XVII Ponce, 1993	364	227	76	61
Pan-American Games*				
V Canada, 1967	49	9	14	26
VI Colombia, 1971	105	30	49	26
VII Mexico, 1975	134	57	45	32
VIII Puerto Rico, 1979	145	64	47	34
IX Venezuela, 1983	176	79	53	44

X United States, 1987	175	75	52	48
XII Argentina, 1995	238	112	66	60
XI Cuba,* 1991	265	140	62	63

Olympic Games**

II Paris, 1900	2	1	1	-
III Saint Louis, 1904	11	5	3	-
VIII Paris, 1924	-	-	-	-
IX Amsterdam, 1928	-	-	-	-
X Los Angeles, 1932	-	-	-	-
XIV London, 1948	1	-	1	-
XV Helsinki, 1952	-	-	-	-
XVI Melbourne, 1956	-	-	-	-
XVII Rome, 1960	-	-	-	-
XVIII Tokyo, 1964	1	-	1	-
XIX Mexico, 1968	4	-	4	-
XX Munich, 1972	8	3	1	4
XXI Montreal, 1976	13	6	4	3
XXII Moscow, 1980	20	8	7	5
XXIII Barcelona,1992	31	14	6	11

* Data taken from the daily *Granma,* August 21, 1991 (medals).
** Data referred only to Olympic Games in which Cuba participated.

SOURCE: National Statistics Committee. Daily *Granma,* Havana, August 21, 1991.

PICTURES, MAPS AND ENGRAVINGS

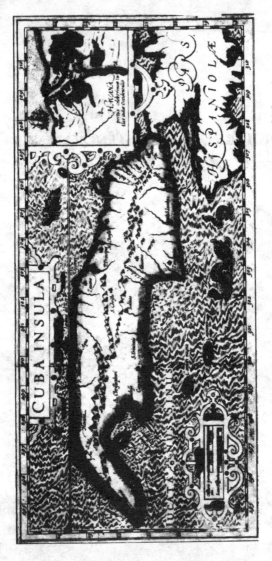

Mercator Geraldi: *Cuba insula*, Asterodami, 1607 (Map collection of the José Martí National Library).

NUESTRA SEÑORA
DE LA ASUNCION
DE BARACOA (1513)

SANTIAGO DE CUBA
(1515)

SAN SALVADOR
DE BAYAMO (1513)

PUERTO PRINCIPE
(1515)

SANCTI SPIRITUS
(1514)

LA SANTISIMA
TRINIDAD (1514)

SAN CRISTOBAL
DE LA HABANA (1514)

The first seven cities founded by the conquistadors during the 16th century.

THE SUGAR INDUSTRY
A. La Cunyaya
B. A primitive *trapiche*
C. A Sugar Mill

Evolution of the sugar industry.

Cuban revolutionary troops charge, armed with machetes during the 1868 and 1895 wars of independence.

Carlos Manuel de Céspedes.

The burning of crops and towns was a weapon used by the Cuban Liberation Army against the Spanish colonial economy.

Generalissimo Máximo Gómez.

Major Ignacio Agramonte.

The Baraguá Protest: the revolutionary intransigence marks the continuation of the struggle for national independence.

General Antonio Maceo.

José Martí.

North-American interference in the Cuban people's war against colonialism, in a bid to thwart its independence (1898).

The neocolonial republic is inaugurated: General Wood and Tomás Estrada Palma during the ceremony to swear the latter into office (1902).

Victims of the concentration of peasants in the cities decreed by the Spanish colonial government.

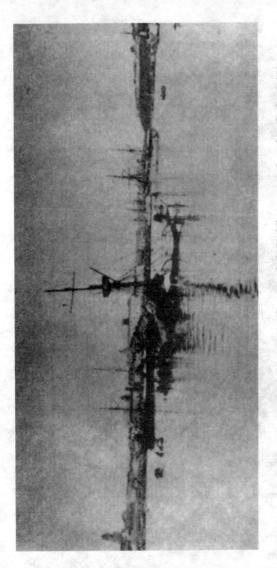

Remains of the North-American battleship *Maine* after it exploded while it was anchored in the bay of Havana.

Julio Antonio Mella.

Rubén Martínez Villena.

Popular demonstration just after Gerardo Machado's government was overthrown (the 1933 Revolution).

Antonio Guiteras Holmes.

Coup d'etat by Fulgencio Batista (March 10, 1952).

Students demonstration against Batista's dictatorship.

Fidel around the time of the assault against the Moncada Garrison.

The yacht *Granma* that brought to Cuba the expeditionaries under Fidel Castro's command, to begin the armed struggle in the mountains (1956).

Commander Camilo Cienfuegos.

Commander Ernesto Che Guevara during the take over of Santa Clara (1958).

The anti-illiteracy campaign after the triumph of the Revolution.

Revolutionary fighters at Playa Girón, the first defeat of US imperialism in the Americas (1961).

Mass rally at Revolution Square.

Session of the First Congress of the Communist Party of Cuba; the Commander-in-Chief and First Secretary of the Party Fidel Castro reads the Report to the Congress (1975).

Working session at the People's Power National Assembly.

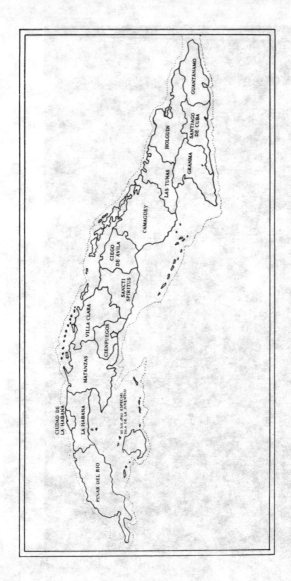

Current political and administrative division of Cuba into provinces.

BIBLIOGRAPHY

Averhoff Purón, Mario. *Los primeros partidos políticos*. La Habana: Instituto Cubano del Libro, 1971.

Cabrera, Olga. *Guiteras, la época, el hombre*. La Habana: Editorial de Arte y Literatura, Instituto Cubano del Libro, 1974.

Cairo Ballester, Ana. *El movimiento de veteranos y patriotas*. (Notes for an ideological review of the year 1923).

Castro, Fidel. *La historia me absolverá*. La Habana: Instituto Cubano del Libro, 1967.

——————. Speech delivered at the United Nations. New York, September 26, 1960.

——————. Centennial commemoration of one hundred years of struggle, October 10, 1968.

——————. Speech delivered at the commemoration of the one hundred anniversary of the fall in combat of Major General Ignacio Agramonte. Camagüey, May 11, 1973.

——————. Speech delivered at the commemoration of the 20th anniversary of the attack against the Moncada Garrison. Santiago de Cuba, July 26, 1973.

——————. Main Report to the First Congress of the Communist Party of Cuba, La Habana, 1975.

——————. *El dilema de la deuda externa y el nuevo orden económico internacional como una alternativa verdadera*. Unabridged text of the interview granted to the Mexican newspaper *Excelsior*. La Habana: Editora Política, 1985.

——————. *Por el camino correcto*. Collection of writings. La Habana: Editora Política, 1987.

——————. *La crisis económica y social del mundo...*, La Habana: Oficina de Publicaciones del Consejo de Estado, 1983.

——————.*La deuda externa*. La Habana: Oficina de Publicaciones del Consejo de Estado, 1985.

CASTRO, RAÚL. Speech delivered at the commemoration of the 8th anniversary of the attack against the Moncada Garrison.

CEPERO BONILLA, RAÚL. *Azúcar y abolición*. La Habana: Editorial de Ciencias Sociales, Instituto Cubano del Libro, 1971.

CISNEROS BETANCOURT, SALVADOR; MANUEL SANGUILY, ENRIQUE JOSÉ VARONA AND JUAN GUALBERTO GÓMEZ. *Antimperialismo y república*. La Habana: Editorial de Ciencias Sociales, Instituto Cubano del Libro, 1970.

COLLAZO, ENRIQUE. *Los americanos en Cuba*. La Habana: Editorial de Ciencias Sociales, Instituto Cubano del Libro, 1972.

——————. *Desde Yara hasta el Zanjón, apuntes históricos*. La Habana: Instituto Cubano del Libro, 1967.

CRUZ, MANUEL DE LA. *Episodios de la Revolución Cubana*. La Habana: Instituto Cubano del Libro,1968.

DEPARTAMENTO DE FILOSOFÍA, UNIVERSIDAD DE LA HABANA. *Pensamiento revolucionario cubano*. La Habana: Editorial de Ciencias Sociales, Instituto Cubano del Libro, 1971.

DEPARTAMENTO DE INSTRUCCIÓN, MINISTERIO DE LAS FUERZAS ARMADAS REVOLUCIONARIAS. *Manual de Capacitación Cívica*, La Habana, n. d.

FIGUEREDO SOCARRÁS, FERNANDO. *La revolución de Yara, 1868-1878*. La Habana: Instituto Cubano del Libro, 1968.

FONER, PHILLIP. *Historia de Cuba y sus relaciones con Estados Unidos*. Vol. 2. La Habana: Editorial de Ciencias Sociales, Instituto Cubano del Libro, 1973.

Franco, José Luciano. *Antonio Maceo, apuntes para una historia de su vida.* 3 vols. La Habana: Editorial de Ciencias Sociales, Instituto Cubano del Libro, 1973.

Gandarilla, Julio César. *Contra el yanqui.* La Habana: Editorial de Ciencias Sociales, Instituto Cubano del Libro, 1973.

Gómez , Máximo. *Diario de campaña, 1868-1899.* La Habana: Instituto Cubano del Libro, 1968.

——————. *El viejo Eduá.* La Habana: Instituto Cubano del Libro, 1968.

González Carbajal, Ladislao. *El Ala Izquierda Estudiantil.* La Habana: Editorial de Ciencias Sociales, Instituto Cubano del Libro, 1974.

Guerra, Ramiro. *Manual de historia de Cuba.* La Habana: Editorial de Ciencias Sociales, Instituto Cubano del Libro, 1971.

——————. *Azúcar y población en las Antillas.* La Habana: Editorial de Ciencias Sociales, Instituto Cubano del Libro, 1976.

——————. *La expansión territorial de los Estados Unidos, a expensas de España y los países hispanoamericanos.* La Habana: Editorial Nacional de Cuba, 1964.

——————. *La Guerra de los 10 Años.* La Habana: Editorial de Ciencias Sociales, Instituto Cubano del Libro, 1972.

Guevara, Ernesto. *Obras, 1957-1967.* 2 vols. La Habana: Casa de las Américas, 1970.

Ibarra, Jorge. *Ideología mambisa.* La Habana: Colección Cocuyo, Instituto Cubano del Libro, 1972.

Instituto de Historia del Movimiento Comunista de la Revolución Socialista de Cuba. *Carlos Baliño. Documentos y artículos.* La Habana: Departamento de Orientación Revolucionaria del Comité Central del Partido Comunista de Cuba, 1976.

Instituto de Historia de Movimiento Comunista y de la Revolución Socialista de Cuba. *El movimiento obrero cubano. Documentos y artículos.* 2 vols. La Habana: Editorial de Ciencias Sociales, 1975, 1977.

JENKS, LELAND. *Nuestra colonia de Cuba.* Buenos Aires: Editorial Palestra, 1959.

LE RIVEREND, JULIO. *Historia económica de Cuba.* La Habana: Editorial Revolucionaria, Instituto Cubano del Libro, 1975.

——————. *La república, dependencia y revolución.* La Habana: Editorial de Ciencias Sociales, Instituto Cubano del Libro, 1975.

——————. *Historia económica de Cuba.* La Habana: Editorial Pueblo y Educación, Instituto Cubano del Libro, 1975.

MARTÍ, JOSÉ. *Obras completas.* La Habana: Editorial de Ciencias Sociales, Instituto Cubano del Libro, 1975.

MENCÍA, MARIO. *Tiempos precursores.* La Habana: Editorial de Ciencias Sociales, 1986.

MIRÓ ARGENTER, JOSÉ. *Cuba, crónica de la guerra, las campañas de invasión y de occidente,* 1895-1896. La Habana: Editorial de Ciencias Sociales, Instituto Cubano del Libro, 1970.

Moncada. Special edition to pay homage to the 20th Anniversary of July 26, 1953. La Habana: Editorial de Ciencias Sociales, Instituto Cubano del Libro, 1973.

MORALES, VIDAL. *Iniciadores y primeros mártires de la revolución cubana.* La Habana: Consejo Nacional de Cultura, 1963.

MORENO FRAGINALS, MANUEL. *El ingenio.* 3 vols. La Habana: Editorial de Ciencias Sociales, 1978.

NÚÑEZ MACHÍN, ANA. *Rubén Martínez Villena.* La Habana: UNEAC, 1971.

ORTIZ, FERNANDO. *Contrapunteo cubano del tabaco y el azúcar.* Las Villas: Dirección de Publicaciones, Universidad Central de Las Villas, 1963.

——————. *Los negros esclavos.* La Habana: Editorial de Ciencias Sociales, Instituto Cubano del Libro, 1975.

PÉREZ DE LA RIVA, JUAN et al. *La república neocolonial.* La Habana: Editorial de Ciencias Sociales, Instituto Cubano del Libro, 1975.

PICHARDO, HORTENSIA. *Documentos para la historia de Cuba*. 3 vols. La Habana: Editorial de Ciencias Sociales, Instituto Cubano del Libro, 1971, 1973.

PINO SANTOS, OSCAR. *Historia de Cuba, aspectos fundamentales*. La Habana: Editorial Nacional de Cuba, 1964.

Playa Girón, derrota del imperialismo. La Habana: Ediciones R., 1961.

PORTUONDO, FERNANDO. *Historia de Cuba*. La Habana: Editora del Consejo Nacional de Universidades, 1965.

PORTUONDO, JOSÉ ANTONIO. *Bosquejo histórico de las letras cubanas*. La Habana: Ministerio de Educación, Dirección General de Cultura, 1960.

RIVERO MUNIZ, JOSÉ. *Tabaco, su historia en Cuba*. La Habana: Instituto de Historia, Comisión Nacional de la Academia de Ciencias de Cuba, 1964.

ROA, RAMÓN. *Pluma y machete*. La Habana: Editorial de Ciencias Sociales, Instituto Cubano del Libro, 1969. (The original edition was entitled *Con la pluma y el machete*).

ROA, RAÚL. *La revolución del 30 se fue a bolina*. La Habana: Editorial de Ciencias Sociales, Instituto Cubano del Libro, 1976.

RODRÍGUEZ, CARLOS RAFAEL. *Cuba en el tránsito al socialismo, 1959-1963*. La Habana: Editora Política, 1979.

ROIG DE LEUCHSENRING, EMILIO. *La guerra libertadora cubana de los treinta años, 1868-1898*. La Habana: Oficina del Historiador de la Ciudad, 1958.

——————. *Historia de la Enmienda Platt*. La Habana: Oficina del Historiador de la Ciudad, 1961.

ROJAS, MARTHA. *La generación del centenario en el juicio del Moncada*. La Habana: Editorial de Ciencias Sociales, Instituto Cubano del Libro, 1973.

SANTAMARÍA, HAYDÉE. "Haydée habla del Moncada," in *26*. La Habana: Editorial de Ciencias Sociales, Instituto Cubano del Libro, 1971.

Siete documentos de nuestra historia. Editora Política. La Habana, 1967.

Soto, Lionel. *La Revolución del 33*. 3 vols. La Habana: Editorial de Ciencias Sociales, 1977.

Un encuentro con Fidel. Interview by Gianni Miná, published by the Oficina de Publicaciones del Consejo de Estado, La Habana, 1988.

Vignier, E. and G. Alonso. *La corrupción política y administrativa en Cuba, 1944-1962*. La Habana: Editorial de Ciencias Sociales, Instituto Cubano del Libro, 1973.